Peak Profit Potential

A 4-Step Program to Stop Your Business from Leaking Money

Donna Marie Thompson PhD

Peak Profit Potential

A 4-Step Program to Stop Your Business from Leaking Money

ISBN: 1936621053
ISBN 13: 9781936621057

DEDICATION

I dedicate this book to all of the amazing business professionals, thought leaders, and visionaries who have helped me to succeed in ways that mere words cannot express. These include: Brian Tracy, Jay Abraham, Jack Canfield, and Dan Kennedy. They go far beyond theory to help others succeed … and I am exceedingly grateful. Thanks for all you do to advance the art and science of business success.

To the hundreds of businesses and clients that I have been fortunate to be associated with; you have formed the foundation for the practical application of the business success and profitability principles in this book.

And to small business owners and entrepreneurs everywhere who are the driving force in creating profitable economic activity that is vital for all of us.

WHAT OTHERS ARE SAYING ABOUT
PEAK PROFIT POTENTIAL

This book is a simple yet powerful road map for entrepreneurial small businesses as they try hard to find a solution to their growth and cash flow, particularly in our fast-moving world today. Use this book as a key resource for training yourself and equipping others in your organization. By the way it's also a valuable topic source for your weekly meetings.
Carlos Dias, coauthor with Jay Abraham of *"The CEO Who Sees Around Corners,"* and *"Creative Leadership for Turbulent Times,"* the eLearning program for CEOs and senior executives

Far too many business books take us on a journey that is so complicated; we are lost before the first turn. In Peak Profit Potential, Donna Marie Thompson has created a simple-to-follow roadmap showing how to do the right things right in your business and putting you back in control. While most businesses tend to think that the road to more revenue is driven on sales, the truth is that your bottom line is also dependent on solid cost-cutting measures and understanding the balance between the two. Donna Marie's focus on "actionable information" helps in getting a full picture of what makes a business tick. This is a superb book,

written with the busy business owner in mind. Definitely one to buy, and apply, and return to over and over again.
~ Peter Hoppenfeld, Attorney, Advisor and Strategist

Donna Marie Thompson has written a ground-breaking book. In Peak Profit Potential, she has provided a practical and proven framework to help rethink strategies for taking any business to the next level. This is the powerful, every-day guidebook to reaching profit goals that doesn't depend on sales and marketing! It's the simple path to boosting the Bottom Line. This information is easy to understand and provides a springboard for strategic planning and cost cutting. A resource to return to over and over.
~ Tommy Antonopoulos, Former District Manager
with Panera Bread

"Peak Profit Potential" is the business school for entrepreneurs that they don't teach in business school! I've suffered an MBA degree, spent 20 years with a Fortune 10 company, and now run my own business and have not come across the practical, specific, actionable business concepts and practices explained as clearly and simply as Donna Marie explains them in this book. This is a "must study" for every small business owner who wants to reach their peak profit potential!
~ Sylvia Henderson, Idea Strategist, Author of *"Hey, That's MY Idea!"*, IdeaSuccessNetwork.com

As a Project Manager, no matter how we look at it, approaching something as important as profits necessitates a plan. If we have a solid plan in place, to employ over and over, at deeper levels, reaching our Peak Profit Potential is a VERY realistic goal. In this book, Donna Marie Thompson has not only carefully laid out a specific, actionable guide, she also has done so with easy-to-use practices and tools that anyone can apply, one step at a time. This is a practical approach to cost cutting and profits that we can only learn in the real world, in the trenches. THIS is what they don't teach us in business school.

~ Camper Bull, PMP

"My father says 'measure twice, cut once' for little projects around the house. So why are so many businesses suffering because they don't even measure once? Donna Marie Thompson makes it easy to measure, even if you hate numbers, or are too busy to care. But you must care because your business is likely hemorrhaging money and you don't even know it ..until you read this book."

~ Justin Hitt, Author of *"How You Can Increase B2B Profits in 90 Days or Less, Guaranteed"*

DISCLAIMER AND/OR LEGAL NOTICES

This book is not intended to provide specific business advice to any person, business owner, or business. While the publisher and author have used their best efforts in preparing this book, they make no representations or warranties with respect to the accuracy or completeness of the contents of this book or supporting materials. Names have been changed for use in the examples and the case studies. The advice and strategies contained herein may not be suitable for your situation. You should consult a professional where appropriate. Neither the publisher nor the author shall be liable for any loss of revenue, profit, or any other commercial damages, including but not limited to special, incidental, consequential, or other damages. The purchaser or reader of this publication assumes full responsibility for the use of these materials and information. Adherence to all applicable laws and regulations, both advertising and all other aspects of doing business in the United State or any other jurisdiction, is the sole responsibility of the purchaser or reader.

PEAK PROFIT POTENTIAL
A 4-Step Program to Stop Your Business from Leaking Money

By Donna Marie Thompson, PhD

Appendix

TABLE OF CONTENTS

INTRODUCTION

Running a business today is quite challenging. There are more pressures than ever before accelerating at a rate never witnessed before. New competitors are emerging all the time from both likely and unlikely places. Big players are moving down market. Small players are moving up market. And customers are more informed than ever with 24-hour access to unlimited information across the globe.

Yesterday's breakthroughs and innovations rapidly become today's common practice. It's tougher than ever to stand out from the crowd. The net effect means that doing the same things in the same ways eventually leads to a profit squeeze. There's a reason that 93% of businesses don't survive their first 10 years. Doing more of the same is not the name of the game; it's the road to ruin.

Therein Lies Opportunity

Yet in all of this business turbulence lie opportunities. Amazing opportunities. While on one hand there are more competitors; on the other hand there are more powerful tools available to help you analyze and

> *...Yet in all of this business turbulence lie **opportunities.***

grow your business. Some of the latest marketing, communication, and social media advances offer great access and value never before possible – that is, when they're carefully aligned with your business strategy.

Today, tens of thousands of business owners and managers are operating right on the edge of profitability. The sad fact is that they believe that's the way it has to be. But there are many ways – both new and old -- to boost profits. There are literally scores of ways to see the light at the end of the tunnel. I learned throughout my international management consulting career the difference between high-level management information that is nice to know, vs. detailed, actionable information that drives profits and strategic processes. The advantages of visibility of the inner workings of the business can be reaped by businesses of all sizes yet it seems that only the big boys are taking full advantage. Routinely, larger businesses capitalize on this and exploit it to the max to gain competitive advantage and to boost profits.

Sadly, not all small businesses will make it. Many simply will not get the message; others are not willing to change their mindset and take the necessary steps. Furthermore, not all owners and managers are ready to do what needs to be done. Some are not prepared for the new competitive reality. Others believe that immediate change is essential, yet for some reason, they still cannot act.

Some business owners are simply stuck and don't know the best moves; they don't know their options. Some don't have the tools. Others can't afford to take another wrong action that takes them even further away from their profit goals. They simply can't spend any more time or money chasing empty promises and following programs that do not work, despite the breathless claims of making a million dollars while you sleep. We've all heard the hype. And that's just what it is. So let's do this the right way. The proven way. Follow the path that works, no matter what. No cookie-cutter solutions here, just powerful tools that work. There are higher and better ways to manage your business and navigate high into the profit zone.

If your business is tracking sideways or downward, unless you do something different, it is only logical to expect more of the same. You need to know what it takes to succeed. Many of the same strategies, principles, and tactics the big boys use will work very well in your business, probably even better because you are more agile and committed.

Awareness, action, and attention to detail is the AAA in business today. You can get unstuck. You <u>can</u> boost profits and overcome many profit challenges in your business, no matter what. It requires a change in thinking. It requires refocusing on your key profit drivers. Do you even know your key profit drivers? You will before you reach the end of *Peak Profit Potential*.

Will you choose to be one of the successful business owners and managers who can master your numbers and reclaim your future?

Profitability Tools

Whether you are a business owner or a department manager, there is no reward in struggling needlessly. The answers are close at hand. Powerful yet simple tools, custom tailored to your business are the answer. The good news is that you don't need to be a math whiz to take advantage of them. A little time, a little attention, and the prize of increased profitability is yours.

✔ Every industry is different so the tools are adaptable.
✔ Every business is different so the tools are flexible.

No matter where your business is now on the profitability continuum, there are always ways to boost your profits. This book offers powerful Peak Profit Potential strategies for business owners and managers to follow on the path to increased profitability. Using the methods presented in this book can result in a 10-30% boost in profits within 60 days. And it's not uncommon for business to double and redouble their profit gains particularly if you focus on key profit drivers. These tools can give you the power to multiply your performance in every aspect of your business in ways you've never done before. You can make better decisions. You can get twice as much done. You can focus on the 20% of activities that generate 80% of the results you're looking for.

Let's revisit the assumptions you made when you started your business. Which of these reasons ring true for you when you started out?

✔ Financial freedom
  • Make more money
  • Independence
  • Retire early

- ✔ Creative freedom
  - Create new offerings
  - Your leadership
  - Try out a new concept
- ✔ Lifestyle freedom
  - Work when you want
  - Get free from your boss
- ✔ Better serve your customers
  - Align closer to their needs
  - Interact in a better way
  - Respond faster to the market
- ✔ Prestige
  - Community
  - Industry
- ✔ Build an asset to sell
  - Serial entrepreneur
  - Create an estate

Are you satisfied with where you are? Or do you want to do better, make more profit, serve more customers, or work fewer hours? Keep these and your other reasons you started your business in mind as you read and implement the tools featured in *Peak Profit Potential.* The extent to which there are gaps between your initial assumptions and your current reality will help you to focus your attention and priorities.

Step-by-Step Guide

This book lays out the step-by-step path to success. You will embark on a journey of steady profit improvement. It's not always about more sales, although more profitable sales are always welcome. It's not simply about cutting costs, although cutting excess costs is a great idea. It's definitely not about working longer and harder, that's what we're trying to avoid. The brute force approach can be effective in the short term. But it's not sustainable in the long term. The Peak Profit Potential strategies focus on doing the right things right in your business and putting you back in control.

In this book, I draw the distinction between strategic attention and operational management attention. Strategic attention can be defined as looking up and out from your business and looking toward the future. Operational attention can be defined as looking down and inside your business.

There are eye-opening assessments and Top 10 lists. There are links to on-line tools. You can get down and dirty with your business – as it is now. But, believe me, your business won't be that way for long. This book will change the way you think about your business. It will even change the way you think about yourself as a business person. As a leader. As an entrepreneur.

Even if you hate numbers, there are easy formulas you can use to gain a clearer picture of what is going on inside your business. To see the gears move. To gain the insights into what is driving profits higher and what is forcing them lower. No cookie-cutter approaches

> *... Even if you hate numbers there are easy formulas you can use to **gain a clearer picture** of what is going on inside your business.*

here; it's all custom. No complex multi-page formulas needed; it's quite simple. Many number phobes begin to take on a new appreciation for a few illuminating business indicators that become their favorites. Others simply rely on their accountant to do the heavy lifting. It works either way.

Taking Action

Read the book from front to back, skim the book first, or dive deep in a particular section. It's all up to you how you get started. What matters most is that you do get started. If you're currently in fire-fighting mode, put out the fire first then regroup to boost your profits. The fact is what separates successful business owners from unsuccessful ones is purposeful and strategic ACTION. Begin with actionable information. Then the resulting action is purposeful, directed, and measureable. It becomes a reinforcing loop. Keep doing what's working and stop doing what isn't. It sounds simple, yet in business, oftentimes it's not without necessary transparency into the inner workings of your business. Not without the underlying information that shows exactly what's going on inside your business…what's making your specific business tick. You will have a new lens through which to view your business. And with increased visibility naturally comes increased profit opportunity. Opportunity that is yours for the taking. Carpe diem.

My promise to you is that by the end of the book you will look at your business like never before. You will see facets you've never seen before. You will see the power of customized business tools and analytics you never realized before. Your numbers and your insights reveal your Peak Profit Potential. You have the power to reshape your business and boost your profits. You also have the power to maintain these profits indefinitely. And you have the power to grow your profits even more over time. Results come from a laser-like focus on implementation. This system has worked for thousands of businesses and it will work for yours too.

This book: presents key business drivers, explains the power of business performance management, introduces **The Profit Pyramid**™, highlights likely areas to check for profit leaks, presents four strategies to stop your business from leaking money today, and provides a guide for continuous profit maximization. Are you ready to boost profits in your business right now? Let's get started.

CHAPTER 1

BUSTING PROFIT MYTHS

It's not what you don't know that kills you;
it's what you know for sure that ain't true. Mark Twain

Tens of thousands of new businesses are started each year – many with the same hopes and dreams. "I want to do things my way" is a common refrain from new business owners. Other reasons I hear are "I'm very solid technically, why should someone else reap the profits from my work?" "People tell me I could make a lot more money on my own."

Whatever the reasons that you got into business, the landscape probably looks very different now from when you started. Massive changes are taking place at a breathtaking pace. Some industries are undergoing seismic shifts in as little as five years. Entire industries have disappeared; for instance how often do you use your phone as a camera?

Where You Are

In the midst of the fast and sweeping changes around you take a look at your business. You probably notice that you are not living the lifestyle you had hoped after a lot of hard work. Maybe you thought you'd be farther down the road by now. Maybe you thought you would have made more progress in your target markets by now. Believe me, you're not alone. When I speak at international conferences, business people tell me all the time that they are struggling. They are working excessively long hours. They spend far too much time away from their families. And they are disappointed that all of their hard work is not paying off. But they keep on doing what they're doing. Working. Wishing. And hoping.

Let's be real. None of us expected that it would be easy to be a successful business owner. But 60-hour work weeks without solid results are growing old and tiresome. Keep doing what you're doing and you'll keep getting what you got….or less. It's time for a change.

Clearly, there has to be a better way. Let's look at some common myths about running a business, and then bust them one-by-one.

Myth 1 – Working Harder is the Answer

If you're working harder, putting in longer hours, making more sales calls, meeting with more customers, it's time to take a step back. It's time to analyze. Do you know which of these activities is really paying off? And I mean paying off in proportion to your time, effort, resources, and capital. An adequate return on total investment is one measure.

Often we can be lulled into thinking things are going well because sales or profits are increasing. Are sales rising across your industry? If they are, are you getting your fair share of the increase? And at what cost? Do your sales increase proportionally to your investment? When profit margins rise proportionally based on the resources that go into generating them, then productivity and efficiency are fully taken into consideration.

Many businesses make a decision to take on a project, to explore new markets, to try out new things. That is the foundation of innovation, and it's a good thing. In the short term it can be quite exciting. Surely, when it all falls into place, this can lead to new products, new services, new ways to bundle offerings, or new markets to enter. Yet over time, an analysis of essential inputs is required to validate whether the specific investment of management attention and resources is paying off as expected. This new effort needs to be assessed in the light of day against all current business opportunities. Is it profitable? Is it sustainable? Is it efficient? Quite simply, is this the best use of scarce time and money?

And extreme price competition is a whole story in of itself. Use extra caution when investing in a non-differentiated commodity business that is totally based on price competition. Often, keeping costs low and riding out the product decline is a limiting strategy in a declining market. Think about creative ways to re-energize the product with differentiation. One question to ask: Will customers be willing to pay for something extra: more options, higher quality, faster delivery, or add-on services, for example?

Myth #1 Case Study

Robert was working 65 hours a week in his printing and graphics business. He was spending more time and money, yet barely maintaining the status quo. His costs were rising and as a result, his profits were squeezed. To keep the cash flowing, he began taking on more graphics design orders, simple low-end work, yet high volume. The short-term objective was to help defray fixed costs and keep cash flowing and make a little money in the process. In the very short term, this type of thinking sometimes can be justified. But the expected profits did not follow. "Make a little money" came back to bite the business; that is exactly what happened.

As it turns out, Robert discovered that even on the low-priced items often there was rework required. In fact, rework was critical to keep the client happy, to get paid, and to get customer referrals. But this experiment was clearly not working from either the profit, or return on assets, perspective. A change in strategy was needed and fast.

> *... change orders became **a profit source** instead of a profit sink and led to a significant source of increased profits.....*

By cutting back on those enticing high-volume, low-profit orders and being more selective, Robert was able to actually increase profits in his business. Avoiding low-margin orders freed up time to do more specialized work, and to get the client requirements fully understood and signed off on. Under this approach, almost no rework was required. In fact, if there was rework, it was completed under a paid change order. Ironically, the bane of graphics designers is change orders. Yet these change orders became a profit source instead of a profit sink and led to a significant source of increased revenue, customer satisfaction, and professional pride. When customers made changes to their agreed design, sanity ruled. They now only made changes they were willing to pay for, whereas before these changes would have been absorbed by Robert's business.

Myth #1 Reflection

Think back over Robert's situation to see what was going on in his business and his *work harder* approach. Next, on to your business. Take a few minutes now to answer these six questions to see how this *working harder* phenomenon is playing out in your business. Even if you are in a different industry in a different market, the *working harder* approach could be at work. The key thought is: is this approach working for you or against you?

- ✔ In what areas of your business have you adopted a *work harder* approach?
- ✔ How did you decide on the activities to be done?
- ✔ How did you measure the impact?
- ✔ What were your results?
- ✔ Is this something to do more of or less of in your business?
- ✔ When is a good time to start to make the needed changes?

The Litmus Test

Working harder is not the answer unless everything you do directly builds customer value and boosts profits. That's the litmus test for everything you do and everything your team and your business does. Working harder is not the answer if it doesn't produce the measurable results you're looking for. Doing the right things right is a better approach.

Myth 2 – Everything You're Doing Needs to be Changed

When a business is struggling it's sometimes difficult to separate what's working from what's not. Most small businesses are a complex collection of a few core activities and many more supporting activities. Over time, the distinction becomes less clear and the dreaded statement: *this is the way we've always done it* is heard in the hallway. Some things you do make money, a lot of money. Other things, maybe not so much. How can you tell? If your numbers are too aggregated, you can't tell with the necessary precision. You might have a feeling about what is profitable, but you can't really tell for sure. This is very common in small businesses and startups.

Perhaps your core products are selling above expectations yet a new product is not; there could be a dozen reasons for the slow uptake. Knowing about it is a good start. If you believe the new product is viable and solves a pressing need for your clients, take a closer look. The weak performance could be caused by breakdowns in the marketing message, targeting, promised benefits, delivery mechanism, or a host of other reasons. Maybe too many costs are being piled on. Perhaps it's a pricing issue. Often there is unwarranted complexity in the business process. Dig into the data. Talk to the marketplace, and reach out to current and prospective clients before making changes or throwing in the towel. How does your new product solve critical customer needs? How does it relate to your core products? How can you deliver it profitably?

Myth #2 Case Study

In Anna's legal transcription business, a simple product adaptation to offer text plus audios and videos brought a commodity business offering back to life. A large insurance company was willing to pay Anna more for formal statements of claimants when they were offered in multiple formats. In troublesome cases, the insurance company found value in both seeing and hearing the claimant statements, in addition to the standard form of verbatim text.

This was a simple, yet effective innovation. Yet because there are low barriers to entry on this technique, competitors will be soon to follow Anna's lead and thus the competitive advantage will be short lived. The innovation was incremental, based on what the business was already offering, with a twist. Anna's customers appreciate her quest for innovation to better serve them and they will be looking for more. Innovation and solid customer service build loyalty. By understanding how your customers actually use your products you are in a better position to fill more of their needs. Often small changes can have a big impact. Get creative. Many things you're doing are probably just fine; others could have great potential for process improvements.

In businesses of all sizes, barriers to entry are falling faster than ever. The moat around your business is getting harder and harder to defend. Entire industries are becoming obsolete – unthinkable just five years ago. Technological advances are leap-frogging the status quo. There is a need to build barriers to the competition but not to over-rely on them to work for more than a few business cycles. How can you make what's working well in your business work even better? That's the question your competitors are asking, and you could be too.

Myth #2 Reflection

Think back over Anna's situation to see what was going on in her business and her simple, incremental innovation. She made only a slight change in what she was doing and it was appreciated by her client. Next, on to your business. Take a few minutes now to answer these six questions to see how change is playing out in your business. The key thought is: What is working so well in your business that it will not be changed and where are fertile areas to explore or incremental or structural improvements?

> ✔ In what areas of your business have you adopted a *steady state* approach?
> ✔ How did you decide on which areas to change or innovate?
> ✔ How did you measure the impact of the change?
> ✔ What were your results?
> ✔ Is this something to do more of or less of in your business?
> ✔ When is a good time to start to make the needed changes?

Fill Customer Needs

Note which activities in your business contribute directly to customer satisfaction and retain those. Many facets of your business can stay just the way they are. Carefully scrutinize activities that do not. Note what products are currently doing well, and those that are not. Are sales increasing? Are profit margins improving or holding steady? If not, alarm bells are ringing. Regard these signals as an opportunity to better identify your customers' needs.

They might not be using your product according to the directions or using it the way you think they are. Will you take the needed action now to revitalize your offerings and thus, your business?

At the core, most businesses revolve around solid offerings that provide valuable benefits to customers. Generally product features tend to expand over time, yet not all customers want or need all features. A menu-based approach with adaptable pricing can distinguish users whose needs are fully met from those who need a little more and are willing to pay for it. These adaptations might come in areas that you had not thought of in the context of convenience, flexibility, timing, risk management, or product staging. Where can your core products solve more of your clients' problems? The more you know the more profitable solutions you can provide. This breeds intense customer loyalty and increases switching costs. Think of the inconvenience of changing your bank. Then apply that logic to your business. How can you get so involved in your client's business that the thought of changing suppliers is quite unappealing to them? Even if things are working well, there might be significant room to boost profits.

Myth 3 – Tracking Profit Drivers is Just Too Complicated

There are hundreds of financial ratios presented in academic books and other financial sources. It can be overwhelming. Yet to run your business successfully, you'll only need to closely monitor a handful of key profit drivers. Within an industry each business is inherently different at the detail level even if they appear to be the same on the surface. Your experience, your product line, and your cost of capital are major differentiators, especially among small businesses. Imagine one business with an attractively priced line of credit and the business next door operating day-to-day on credit cards at 24% interest. Big difference.

You can't tell from the outside. Who has flexibility? Who has staying power? Who can survive through a temporary lull in sales? Who has the stamina to not only fight off new competitors but also to expand? It's important to look at what activities drive your business success. It's important to look at your numbers. And the good news is that it's easier than you think. As in all businesses, there are a few major profit drivers in your business as well. These drivers are often linked to time, materials, capital, equipment, and after-sales servicing. What makes your business tick? What value does your business offer to the marketplace?

Numbers are not collected for numbers sake. The only reason, other than tax reporting, to collect solid financial data is to support management decision making. Many businesses can benefit by carefully tracking their variable costs. Simply, what does it take to get one order out the door? For example, numbers can help you to decide how to make important decisions in your business.

Should you:	Could you:
Take an order	Add a worker
Raise prices	Add a customer
Remove a customer	Add a product
Add equipment	Offer guarantees

Myth #3 Case Study

Paula is a florist and runs a successful retail shop with a great location on the edge of the city. She gets walk-in traffic for casual arrangements or loose flowers, phone-in orders from the local community, and she also receives orders from national flower service chains. Paula wants to know more about how her business works, yet she doesn't have either the time or the interest for complicated analyses. As in most businesses, costs for the flower shop are incurred at many steps in the process. The phone rings and a large order comes in. What's involved? There is the time to take the order; collect all of the materials including the flowers, vase, nutrients, and water; and then to design the arrangement. Then there is the packaging, delivery, and after-sales servicing if needed. That one order is an example of variable costs in action.

Costing the full order chain is critically important in Paula's business and in yours as well. Perhaps the most important of Paula's profit drivers involve purchasing quality flowers at favorable prices. A second important profit driver is marketing, especially around holidays where Paula is increasingly bumping up against supermarkets as competitors due to their convenience and ability to spur impulse buying through attractive in-store displays.

Paula's costs also include her facility, equipment, energy, property taxes, and other costs that cannot be directly linked to this specific order. These are considered fixed costs; at least they're fixed in the short term. Whether or not this order is filled, there is rent to pay, refrigeration units to run, and other costs that do not vary with each order. Paula has now simplified her approach to focus first on three profit drivers: purchasing, marketing, and delivery. And after she explores the power of this information, she can come back around later and take another look at her other profit drivers and the way they interact with each other.

Retail is one of the industries that is rich with standard metrics that you can begin with: sales per square foot, inventory turns, overall gross margin, and a dozen others. Yet even in retail, there are businesses that are in the dark about their specific numbers. They cannot clearly see what is going on in their business shelf-by-shelf or square foot-by-square foot.

Myth #3 Reflection

Think back over Paula's situation to see what was going on in her business and the perceived complexity of obtaining useful management information. Paula has lots going on in her retail operation. But where exactly do her profits come from? Next, on to your business. Take a few minutes now to answer these six questions to see what information is available and how it be-ing used in your business. The key thought is: What is the main driver of your profits?

✔ What business processes drive increased profits?
✔ What business processes drain your profits?
✔ How much do you really know about your core processes?
✔ How do you measure a process that contributes to profits?
✔ Is there something to do more of or less of in your business?
✔ When is a good time to make the needed changes?

Simple Financial Analysis

When you're looking for numbers in your business, tax returns are a good place to start. Or a monthly income statement has key data as well. Never fear, you can always seek guidance from your accountant. There are lots of sample templates and calcu-lators available. Look for ones that are tailored for your industry and your business. Spreadsheets make quick work of simple fi-nancial analyses and they also have the power to identify and track trends. When you know what you're looking for, then you can drill down into the real meat of the matter.

Just a few simple financial ratios that you handpick can shed enormous light and provide needed visibility into the inner work-ings of your business; it doesn't have to be complicated. As you get comfortable with these ratios, you can adapt them as needed to better align with your decision making requirements. These numbers will reflect a single point in time. Other important infor-mation can be collected over time as the numbers begin to form meaningful trends. When combined, they hold the true power of management information for sound decision making in your business.

In the beginning it's important to be involved in designing ways you will use financial information to monitor your business. Your accountant or your team can pitch in on the design stage. After the metrics are set, it's best for them to be automated to provide you with a simple dashboard where you can quickly and easily compare your results from month to month.

Myth 4 - It Works for other Businesses but It Won't Work for You

Another common myth is that your business is so different that results, time, and productivity can't be measured as successfully as they are measured in other businesses. This is a particularly dangerous myth because it sets your business on a dangerous path where your operations are not closely monitored and measured. Resist all temptation to let yourself off the hook because "your business is different". Every business is indeed unique. Yet at the core, all businesses are the same; they seek to provide in-demand offerings to their customers at a profit. The solution is to accommodate your unique business by tailoring standard financial ratios and custom analyses to meet your management decision-making needs.

After you've selected ratios that are meaningful to your business, they'll be a useful guide to keep your business running comfortably in the profit zone. The unique characteristics of your business can be captured in custom ratios designed specifically for your business. In many cases, only minor adjustments are needed in the formulas to help you track exactly what's happening to your revenues, costs, and profits. Visibility is the name of the profitability game. As it turns out most businesses have more in common than you might think. Don't let this myth stand in the way of you measuring the vital statistics of your operation. Any valid insight is better than operating in a black box environment.

Myth #4 Case Study

Charles was an executive consultant providing a variety of services including: strategy development, operations support, training, and project management. In fact, he did whatever the client needed as long as they paid his rates. When exploring the possibility of using ratio analysis in his business Charles was reluctant at first. He believed that there was no pattern in his services. Some jobs he provided at fixed price, others on an hourly arrangement, and still others a blend of the two with some products included in the mix. When looking to analyze his profitability, Charles discovered that the hourly work was the most profitable, yet the smallest part of his business. Profits were boosted even further when his clients also purchased his products.

Yet increasingly, his clients were trying to manage the risk of cost overruns by seeking more fixed-price work. They wanted round after round of changes but were not so eager to pay for them. Based on this analysis, Charles tightened up his contracts, increased his rates in the fixed price work, added in attractively priced products. This met the needs of both firms. Without this powerful yet simple analysis, Charles was foregoing significant profit potential in his business. He didn't realize how much his hourly rate was being compromised by doing fixed-price work that didn't fully accommodate the unexpected. Charles learned to expect the unexpected and successfully boosted his profits.

Myth #4 Reflection

Think back over Charles' situation to see what was going on in his business and his assertion that he cannot track all of the unexpected twists and turns in his business. Charles offers a wide array of services. But he's not sure which activities are paying off and which are not. And then there are client expectations to think about as well. Next, on to your business. Take a few minutes now to answer these six questions to see what will work in your business and what will not. The key thought is: What do you need to know?

- ✔ What do each of your products and services actually cost?
- ✔ Does your current pricing fully reflect these costs?
- ✔ Under what circumstances do you face cost pressures?
- ✔ Where is there re-work or waste in your business? Why?
- ✔ Is there something to do more of or less of in your business?
- ✔ When is a good time to make the needed changes?

Drill Down

Even in a business where there appears to be no pattern, there is often an underlying pattern in the data that financial ratios can detect. Take it on as a challenge to identify a few core ratios that illustrate the key profit drivers of your business in areas where you have been puzzled in the past.

Myth 5 - It Will Make Me Dependent on Outside Advice Forever

Most small business owners are fiercely independent and aren't keen to take on long-term commitments for outside help. By using this Peak Profit Potential program, you remain in full control. Working with your banker, accountant, or other advisors for only as long as needed avoids long-term dependency. Any consultant worth their fee seeks to empower you to do it yourself. *Teach them to fish* should be the mantra for anyone you bring in to work with you on your business. Business intelligence has been the purview of the big boys for more than 20 years. Simple, yet powerful business intelligence tools have emerged for business-es of all sizes, including the solo entrepreneur.

Several of the standard off-the-shelf accounting and bookkeep-ing packages are suitable for this. (See the *Top 10 Tools for Small Business Management Reporting* plus other helpful lists in the back of the book.) There are also a wide variety of simple busi-ness calculators available for free on the web. Many of these tools are practical and powerful. MS-Excel's data representation capabilities are also expanding rapidly and impressively to help you chart more of your business trends over time.

Many small business owners optimize their encounter with con-sultants and service providers by seeking outside advice only for special situations or to answer a specific question. It's best not to rely on highly-paid outsiders too heavily for the routine operation of your business. When I was working in international consulting, one of my clients was paying a high-powered "guru" $5,000 a day. Yet the contract went on and on. If consultants command high rates, demand proven results and fixed comple-tion dates. Then be done with them, and do it on your own after the strengthened business process improvements are in place and paying their own way.

Myth #5 Case Study

Sandra is a nurse practitioner and sees patients in two different doctor's offices. She was very busy yet not sure she was making the best use of her time. Sandra was frequently taking work home. She didn't know where to begin to assess what was the best use of her time. Sandra took a course on productivity for professionals and sought help from her accountant and a consultant to determine the value of an hour of her time, the cost of an hour of her time, and the typical uses of her time. Sandra discovered that she was spending far too much time on record keeping for which she was not being adequately paid. Armed and empowered with her numbers, Sandra and the consultant worked out new ways to provide all of the essential information required for complete medical records without working a lot of unpaid overtime by reducing her time devoted to recording optional information. Sandra is now equipped to continue monitoring her productivity on her own. After her initial investment, Sandra has all she needs to keep increasing her productivity and profitability. She can seek help again when and if she wants it, but she does not need to.

Myth #5 Reflection

Think back over Sandra's situation to see what is going on in her business; she's trying to do a good job for her clients and meet her professional responsibilities. Sandra is in health care and is highly committed to quality. But she is burning up a lot of her free time doing what she thinks she must do. Next, on to your business. Take a few minutes now to answer these six questions to see what activities are demanding excessive time and resources and where some outside help might be appreciated. The key thought is: What help do you need to identify business processes in your business that can be simplified with no Impact on quality?

> ✔ What product or service seems to be difficult to finish on time?
> ✔ What is the source of the scope creep?

✔ What control steps have you tried that haven't worked?
✔ Are you exceeding a minimum professional or technical standard?
✔ How would you define the problem to an outside consultant?
✔ What would a good solution look like?

Get Only the Help You Need

When defining your profit drivers, variable costs, fixed costs, and other elements of your business, it's OK and often advisable to seek outside help. You have a technical skill that drives your business; you might not have been exposed to the productivity and profitability mindset in your business experience. That is, before now. When talking to outside experts, specify the results that you expect. Ask them to describe their deliverable and show you examples of the level of detail you can expect. Write out the agreed terms in the contract. When it's time to implement, make sure the tools work in your business before you issue the final payment. Seek help in manageable bites. Get a tool, implement it, master it, and track your progress. Most reputable consultants will appreciate your clarity and specificity; it makes their job much easier. And you will get a better, more cost-effective result for your business. There is no need to be totally dependent upon consultants; I know, I am one. On the other hand, there is no reason to avoid them when you need them to help your business.

Myth 6 - Your Competitors are Way Ahead of You

Even if it sounds like you're late to the game, it really doesn't matter. What matters is that you're ready to begin today; the future of informed business decision making awaits you. It is right on the horizon, your horizon. The fact is that many businesses track a multitude of numbers only to satisfy outside interests. They prepare statements for their bankers; provide sales information for their accountants; and gather numbers to prepare local, state, and federal taxes. None of this information is designed to help you manage your business; and certainly not to boost your profits. In fact, a large percentage of businesses measure the wrong things as they, acting on autopilot, push for higher and higher sales without due regard to the *profitability* of those sales. More sales is not the answer; increasingly profitable sales is the answer.

So even if it appears from the outside that others have good visibility into their businesses and that they have a full understanding of their cost and profit drivers, it probably isn't true. Small business owners approach me all the time when I'm speaking at conferences and share that they focus only on their income statement and their bottom line. Sure that's a good starting point, but many business owners don't understand their cost structure across their processes, products, services, customers, and locations. My goal is for you to be one of the few small business owners who champion business analytics, get the information you need, take the appropriate actions, and leave your competition in the dust.

Myth #6 Case Study

One example of using the wrong indicators to measure performance is the length of an average hospital stay. Many hospitals are under increasing pressure from insurers to discharge patients quickly; too quickly as it turns out. This has become particularly problematic with seniors on Medicare. For years, 19% of patients were readmitted with the same condition within 30 days – a bad outcome. When penalties were put in place to discourage avoidable readmissions, Shaddie Brooke Hospital had major incentives to rework their metrics. To improve overall outcomes, some patients were kept as in-patients for longer periods of time, others were assigned dedicated outpatient coordinators, and all were given much clearer, written discharge instructions, often including a pre-scheduled appointment with their own doctor to follow up. Shaddie Brooke's original metrics minimized in-patient days but ultimately led to serious and unnecessary health complications. The new metrics provide better financial and better health care outcomes - a true win-win. Tracking the wrong things not only wastes time it can also be a profit drain …or much worse as this case powerfully illustrates. Now, with the new measures in place, patients were given far superior care as a result and readmission penalties approached zero.

Myth #6 Reflection

Think back over the hospital's situation to see what's really going on. They had metrics; they were actively measuring and tracking indicators. Things looked good from the outside; other hospitals might have thought that Shaddie was out in the lead in terms of performance measurement. But in fact they were far from it. Next, on to your business. It doesn't matter what other businesses like yours are measuring unless it is the right things. Take a few minutes now to answer these six questions to see what activities are true measures for you. The key thought is: What indicators will tell you precisely what you need to know about your business?

✔ What indicators are you currently using?
✔ What indicators are your most successful competitors using?
✔ To what extent do your indicators support strategic decision making?
✔ Where do they fall short?
✔ What else do you need to know?
✔ What steps will you take to refine your indicators?

It's Not Too Late

Now that you know that financial ratios can be simple, yet powerful, it's time to get started. It's not too late. Maybe your competitors are doing it all wrong; maybe they are doing it right. What matters most is what you measure and how you measure it. Now is the perfect time to boost your profits by discovering your underlying business factors through decision-oriented financial analysis. Wouldn't you agree?

Myth 7 - It Will Take a Huge Investment of Money

Many small business owners avoid tracking their operating numbers because of the high perceived cost. They rationalize: *If it works it must be expensive, right*? Well, it could be costing you a lot more to not know your numbers than to make an investment in the tools and techniques needed to keep you fully abreast of your business operations. Many simple packages and spreadsheets do the job just fine. And some of the best vendors are moving their tools down market providing you with a unique opportunity to use the tools the big boys use. Business is business. Profits are profits. Excess costs are excess costs. The tools can help you to tell the story of what is going on in your business.

Myth #7 Case Study

Allen's media and image consulting firm was expanding rapidly on a shoestring budget. His recent marketing efforts and investments were beginning to pay off in increased sales, yet for some reason, cash was still tight. The time lag between new sales and actually receiving payment was a couple of weeks. Allen wanted to get started right away to set up indicators to begin tracking his major variables. His goal was to compare marketing costs with sales and profits over time. Allen began his analysis in an Excel worksheet and then started to track his information in another package. Allen began tracking factors on leads, contacts, conversions, contracts, completion, and payments. He never knew that he was converting 3% of his leads to contracts. He began to pre-qualify more leads to better align his target customer base. One action was to start an active, systematic referral campaign so that his best customers recommended him to others which significantly boosted his conversions. And that was just the beginning. He drilled down on his accounts receivable and took action on the slow payers. Once he got started Allen was a convert to a program to easily and inexpensively discover more and more of the hidden profit potential in his business.

Myth #7 Reflection

Think back over Allen's business to see what was really going on and where he had needed visibility and where he did not. Allen quickly discovered the tremendous power of information to boost his profits. Next, on to your business. Take a few minutes now to answer these six questions to see what you can do quickly and easily in your business. The key thought is: What information do you currently have that makes a difference?

✔ What information do you collect now on a monthly basis?
✔ What actions do you take based on this information?
✔ Where do you note gaps in your knowledge?
✔ What else can you track with your current system?
✔ What do you need to know about the capabilities of your system?
✔ What steps will you take to use your system more fully or replace it?

The good news is that if you are not satisfied with what you have, there are more than a dozen or so packages that provide affordable business intelligence information; no need to break the bank. The secret is to get started with performance measurement of your business on a basic level and expand only as you see fit. The more you look, the more you learn.

Start Small

Start small and build upon a solid foundation after you have a better idea of your information requirements. It's fun and highly profitable. Getting it right is important, but it does not require a huge financial investment. And it will continue to pay dividends month after month in your business as you monitor your operations and your costs, improve your decision making, and boost your profits. If you need help ask your accountant or you can search on *odesk.com* or *elance.com* or other similar service sites. Have your templates customized and built for your needs at a value price. Often it requires a single set up and some testing to make sure everything works as expected. Templates and tools can often easily be modified over time as things change in your business or industry. You don't need to break the bank to get the management information you need right now to significantly boost profits in your business.

Myth 8 - It Will Take a Huge Amount of your Scarce Time

"It takes too much time" is a common refrain among harried small business owners. "I'm too busy selling and delivering to stop and take a look at my numbers, besides I'm profitable. What else do I need to know?" Well, congratulations on being profitable, an important first step in a sound business. Yet profitability is only the beginning. The refining concepts of efficiency and productivity come into play as you expand. Keeping the operation tightly managed is the guiding principle toward profitable and sustainable growth in your business. If your costs are increasing in direct proportion to your volume you're likely missing important economies of scale in operating your business. How can you increase your volume while lowering your average costs per unit? Time spent looking into this will likely save you tons of time and money.

Myth #8 Case Study

Barbara runs a professional organizing business and works with many subcontractors to take on larger and larger jobs. This business strategy was working to lift her above the crowd facing ferocious price competition. But she wasn't sure exactly what was going on in her business. She wasn't tracking business performance; basically she was only tracking her cash. But she could not clearly see the backlogs or the pinch points or the profit killers in her business. To give her a clearer view, Barbara set up a new performance management system with an easy-to-use dashboard. She now spends approximately 20 minutes a day reviewing what's coming in, what's going out, and tracking any delays in orders or payments. This is all the time she needs to stay on top of her business. After the initial set up, it now runs as a management-by-exception system giving Barbara the information she needs and when she needs it. It actually saves her time in the process. And it has turned her business around. Armed with essential information about her business, Barbara is free to pursue larger, more lucrative orders.

Myth #8 Reflection

Think back over Barbara's business to see what was really going on. Barbara was too busy to keep running her business in the dark. Doing more of the same was simply not an option. Barbara's new system revealed valuable information to boost her profits. Next, on to your business. Take a few minutes now to answer these six questions to see what you can do to save time as you grow your business profits. The key thought is: If you only had 20 minutes to spend on management information in your business, what would you look at?

✔ How much time do you spend managing your overall business?
✔ How much time compiling additional information to make decisions?
✔ How much time looking for missing information?
✔ How satisfied are you with your management results and efficiency?
✔ How might you better allocate your management time?
✔ What steps will you take to use your time more effectively?

Only a Few Minutes a Day

There is unparalleled power in accurate management information. Automated systems are essential to time and cost savings along with better information to support informed decision making in your business. When the system is up and running, you can set automatic alert flags for downward trends in sales and profits and upward trends in costs and complaints. After the system is up and running, others can monitor the outputs for exceptions that need to be brought to your attention. In just minutes per day, the time you spend on detailed management of your business will pay off in increased insights and new ways to boost profits. Dan Kennedy championed the phrase: *good enough*. You're not looking for the Mercedes of tools or management information. When you make the commitment to manage your numbers for increased business profits, remember the *good enough* philosophy.

Most successful business owners set aside a specific time after the periodic numbers are in and their dashboard information is prepared. They quickly review the trends, note any variances and exceptions, and take appropriate action. It doesn't take long yet it has a powerful impact on your business and your decision making. Consistency is key. Noting the trends and taking action is where the real gold is.

CHAPTER 2

BUT I HATE NUMBERS

I have learned the novice can often see things that the expert overlooks. All that is necessary is not to be afraid of making mistakes, or of appearing naive. Abraham Maslow

One of the most frequent reasons I hear from business owners to not get started on boosting profits in their business, is "I hate numbers." If you're one of those people I assure you that 6th grade arithmetic is all you need. Sure, you can get fancy and run complex trending and sophisticated co-variant analyses, but that's not necessary to get exactly the information you need.

The good news is that a few simple formulas and ratios, hand-picked for your business, is all you need to get started. They can be presented in user-friendly graphics so you can spot major trends visually. A couple of strategically relevant metrics are all you need. In fact, less is more. Tracking too many dimensions of your business causes you to lose sight of the critical success factors that drive your profits. Focus is the primary attribute here. Selectivity is the watch word for accurately measuring key performance indicators in your business. Don't make this harder than it has to be.

Business Process Exploration

Let's explore: where do profits come from? Across all industries: manufacturing, retail, and professional service providers, there are a myriad of business processes involved. These nine processes are generally present in some form or another:

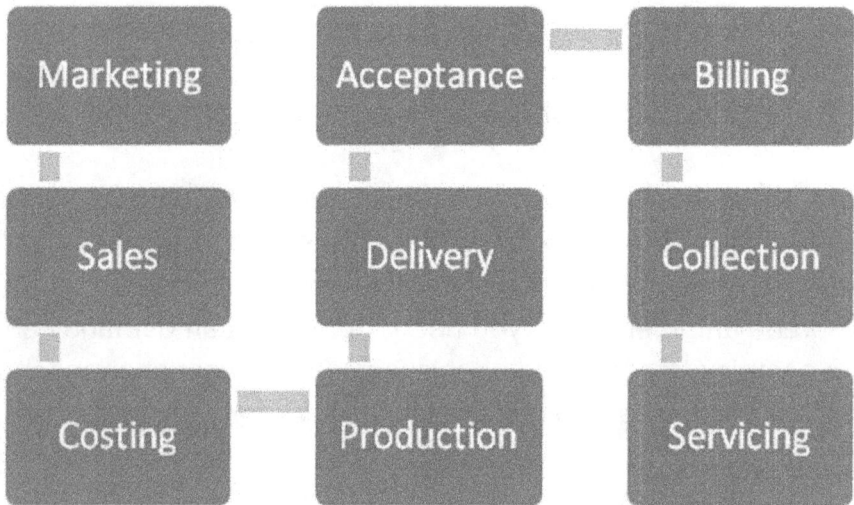

Marketing	Acceptance	Billing
Sales	Delivery	Collection
Costing	Production	Servicing

Within each of these business processes there are associated costs; some are far more complex than others. In each business the steps and associated costs tend to vary greatly. Yet at the same time lies the opportunity for enhanced value creation. Within each of these business processes, at one or multiple levels, lie cost contraction and profit expansion opportunities. If you're wondering where to start, the answer awaits all around you in your business processes. As you take a step back from your daily activities you'll realize that you know dimensions and nuances of your business that no one else knows. You know your customers; you know the marketplace. You have some idea as to what's working and what's not. And there's no shortage of people who are ready, willing, and able to give you candid feedback if you simply ask for it.

Use these nine sample processes to think creatively about the major processes in your business. Are any of these nine general processes the right place for you to start? If so, drill down on the most important one. If not, what business process do you think holds the most hidden profit potential for you?

As you dig deeper into your core processes, simple yet powerful tools aid your decision making. Cost cutting might be high on your list. Many businesses have excess costs; they tend to build up over time and don't generally command your attention when things are simply rolling along. The slow silent accumulation of excess costs helps them to avoid detection. That is, until now.

Many businesses only look at their costs when there is an issue, a sales decline or a profit squeeze.   Yet the most profitable businesses systematically look at their costs and trends on a regular basis. After you look at ways to cut excess costs, the next step is to survey your business for areas to streamline. After a close look, even essential activities might be less efficient than they could be. Everything is on the table when it comes to cutting excess costs, delivering higher quality products, and satisfying customers.

A Few Key Financial Ratios

Here are a few ratios that can provide quick visibility into your business. Ratios come in all different shapes and sizes and can be made to be quite complex; my intent is to keep it simple. Why not peel back the layers to see what's really going on in your business as shown by objective data?

Select an important product or process in your business to begin. Drill down, explore, and repeat. After you start using the analyses that best suit your business, you'll have visibility into multiple layers of your business and the essential information you need to boost your profits quickly and significantly.

Each type of ratio analysis is used for a specific purpose; think of a formula as a tool. A hammer has one purpose, while a screwdriver has another. Same concept. Ratios can be made quite complex, yet there are many simple ways to apply them. Here are four fundamental types of ratios that encompass most of what you'll be working with in your business:

✔ *Liquidity Ratios*
  • Measures your ability to meet your short-term obligations
✔ *Leverage Ratios*
  • Measures the proportion of debt in your financing
✔ *Activity Ratios*
  • Measures how effectively you are using your resources
✔ *Profitability Ratios*
  • Measures returns on sales and investments

A few examples will illustrate how these ratios are generally used.

Liquidity Ratio Example.   Sam is a speech pathologist and he's having more trouble than usual in meeting his bill-paying deadlines. Let's use a liquidity measure called the "quick ratio" to see what's going on with Sam's bills. First, the formula for the quick ratio.

$$\text{Quick ratio} = \frac{\text{current assets- inventory}}{\text{current liabilities}} = \frac{30,000}{32,000} = .94 \quad \text{Target} > 1.1$$

From Sam's balance sheet, he looks at his current assets: they include $7,000 in cash, $10,000 in securities, $13,000 in accounts receivable, and $20,000 in equipment inventories. We'll ignore inventories for now. From Sam's balance sheet, he looks at his current liabilities: they include $30,000 in accounts payable, $1,000 in notes payable, and $1,000 in provision for taxes.

Enter the numbers into the quick ratio formula. So at $30,000 divided by $32,000, Sam's quick ratio equals 0.94 causing a cash squeeze when the target is to keep the quick ratio above 1.1 to ensure that there are more current assets than current liabilities at all times. Sam needs more cash. Maybe Sam cannot pay his bills because he's not collecting fast enough from his customers. If that's true, his customers' cash squeeze has just become Sam's cash squeeze. He needs to boost his quick ratio, and fast.

Leverage Ratio Example.   Caroline is a retailer who sells vintage clothing. In the go-go years, all was going so well that she expanded her business by increasing her floor space and adding to her inventory by taking on some new debt. Let's use a measure called "times interest earned" to track Caroline's leverage.

$$\text{Times interest earned} = \frac{\text{profit before taxes} + \text{interest charges}}{\text{interest charges}} = \frac{160,000}{40,000} = 4 \quad \text{Target} > 8$$

From Caroline's income statement, she looks for the profit before taxes at $120,000 and interest charges of $40,000. So using the formula Caroline's times interest earned ratio equals 4, where the target is 8 times or more. The goal is to ensure that there are plenty of profits to cover the debt service. Caroline either took on too much debt or else her profits have fallen below where it is advised to carry that level of interest obligations. She needs to decrease her interest charges, boost her profits, or both to a more comfortable and sustainable ratio.

Activity Ratio Example. Mike is a construction engineer who designs complex projects and then bids on the components of the job on which his firm can complete profitably. Completing the job on time is one thing; getting paid on time is altogether a different matter. Mike sells $1,440,000 per year, which when divided by 360 days per year translates to $4,000 in sales per day. His receivables are listed on his balance sheet at $160,000. In his contract terms, Mike expects to be paid within 21 days. Let's use a measure called "average collection period" to track this activity measure.

$$\text{Average collection period} = \frac{\text{receivables}}{\text{sales per day}} = \frac{160,000}{4,000} = 40 \quad \text{Target} < 21 \text{ days}$$

Mike's customers are taking almost twice as long to pay him as stipulated in his contracts. Mike needs to accelerate his collections, add more milestones, or perhaps collect down-payments on some jobs.

Profitability Ratio Example. Alice runs a specialized packaging company that ships sales booth signage, equipment, and information materials for hi-tech firms. Her business is doing quite well now that she has added sequential drop-shipments to her mix of offerings. Rather than shipping materials back to HQ, they can be stored temporarily then forwarded directly to the next convention. Alice sells $7,000,000 per year. Her net profit after taxes is $700,000. Let's use a ratio called "profit margin" to track this profitability measure. As it turns out, Alice is underperforming her target profit margin by 2%. Options include: bundling offerings, new offerings, cutting costs, increasing prices, and adding partners, among others.

$$\text{Profit margin} = \frac{\text{net profit after taxes}}{\text{sales}} = \frac{700,000}{7,000,0000} = 10\% \quad \text{Target} >12\%$$

Alice is currently beating the industry average of 8%, yet she is always looking for ways to grow.

Your Business Data

Even if you hate numbers, you can proceed through your business operation systematically to review what is actually happening vs. what you thought was happening. Assess whether liquidity, leverage, activity, or profitability analyses are a good place to start. There's no one right answer; getting started somewhere is what's important. Give it a go and see where the data takes you. If you need more data, see where you can collect it easily and consistently. Test your assumptions. Go deeper if your data doesn't seem to make sense. Maybe there is a large discrepancy between what you thought your costs were vs. what they actually are. And what your profits are vs. what you thought they were after all costs are factored in. It can be quite simple. If you don't have time, seek out your banker, accountant, or trusted business advisor.

As you apply and implement simple measures you will gain significant insights about your business. But don't stop there; the process can be repeated. After you boost profits in one area of your business, you can either move to a new area or else apply additional formulas to the same area to dive deeper. Profit maximization is a continuous process used by only the most successful business people. And after all, isn't that the club you want to be in?

Follow the Path

If you're tired of cookie-cutter advice that doesn't seem to work in your business, the 4-step Peak Profit Potential program will show you the way. Most of the formulas you need generally involve only three or four numbers. Most use simple division. Standard templates and on-line calculators that can be modified to suit your business are generally available to guide you; tools referenced in this book are available at *http://www.PeakProfitPotential.com.*

Graphics can be a big help to aid in your understanding of the information. After the data is in and the core analyses that provide insights into your business are identified, most of these can be translated into very powerful visual images using pie charts, bar charts, trend lines, and other representations to demonstrate the point. You can see the trends over time and use them to make better, more-informed business decisions. In the chart, look at

Product 2. Is the peak in Q2 and the drop in Q3 attributable to seasonality alone or is something else altogether going on? How do you know?

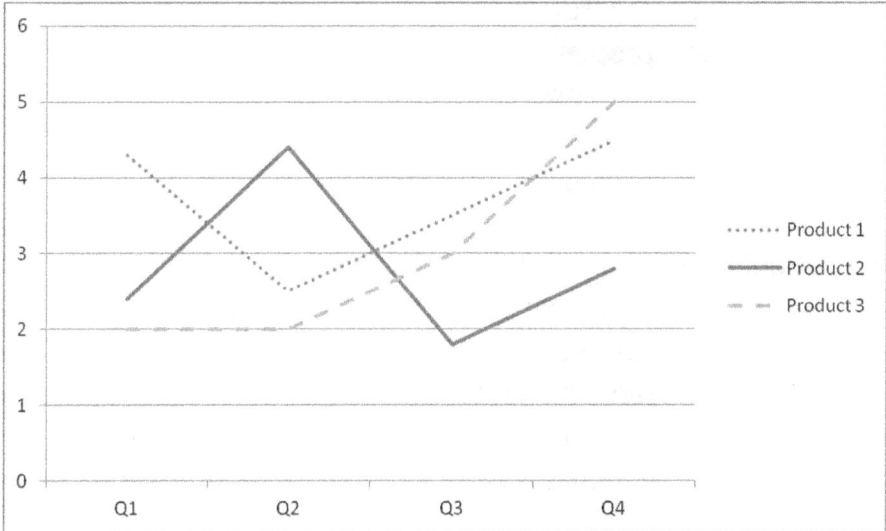

Don't let numbers stand in the way of your dreams for your business. Your dreams for your life. Your freedom. You got to where you are by doing what you had to do. By the time you read to the end of this book you will see the power of increased analytics and increased profits to change everything in your business. And the spillover effects on your life will be dramatic. I've seen it happen scores of times in my consulting career. It's true that knowledge, skillfully applied, is power.

If I told you that managing your numbers for only one hour a week could boost your profits, wouldn't you agree to spend that hour with me right here, right now? Sure, you'd jump at the chance if you believed that it was true. Well, it is true. You may never come to love numbers, and you don't need to. But you will learn to respect their power. Managing your numbers will lead to a life of:

- ✔ Less pressure
- ✔ Informed decision making
- ✔ Improved problem solving
- ✔ Improved investments
- ✔ Better customer service
- ✔ More family time

In the beginning, it's important for you to be fully involved to guide and inform the process of selecting the core business analytics for your unique business. After all, it's your business. After you get it set up, tested, and working, you can delegate the routine analyses to others so you, through your systems, are looking at the same things month after month to effectively track the trends that matter.

Doing the right things right depends on a clear view into the nuts and bolts of your business. In many ways, your business is like every other business. You offer products and services in an attempt to make a profit. Yet at its heart, your business is completely unique – one of a kind. So the way you measure your business and your numbers can be custom tailored to you and your specific needs. Your numbers can meet you where you are now. And they can change as your business changes. And the good news is that you can do it yourself. Quickly and easily.

No need to be dependent upon expensive consultants for long periods of time. I know, I made my living as one. No need for long-term arrangements where it seems that you lose control of your business. Get what you need to know and then you can do it yourself. Or you can work with your banker and your accountant if you prefer. The point is just a few numbers is all you need to effectively boost your profits and consistently track your business. Simple is better. Consistency is key.

CHAPTER 3

KEY BUSINESS DRIVERS

If we don't change our direction, we are likely to end up where we are headed. Chinese Proverb

In any situation, there are a few critical factors that you need to succeed. Without them, you might survive for a while, but if you don't have what you need, you simply will not achieve your goal. This chapter tells a story and then explores business planning activities to help you identify what you know and what you don't know about the cost, value, and profit drivers in your business.

Reach the Peak

Imagine that you've had a long-term goal of climbing Mt. Everest. You're very ambitious; your goal was to reach the highest peak that you could conceivably reach. And now the time has come; your time has come. It's somewhat unbelievable yet here you are at base camp above Kathmandu, quite an achievement in itself. Your head is filled with visions of victory and accomplishment; ah, the view from the summit will be glorious indeed. You are ready to do what it takes, no matter what it takes. At 5am it's time to move, to advance, and to play big. As always, you're well prepared. Sure, it's cold but it's just as you expected. You're equipped. This is just what you've trained for months and endless months. The landscape looks familiar because you've seen it over and over in your mind. Then it is time; the journey is about to begin. You embark on the trek of your life. Slow and steady, step by step the first hour passes as you progress up the mountain.

As you climb higher and higher, the air is getting thinner and thinner. The sun is bright and the glare is intense, but for some reason, the sun is not sharing its warmth. Three more hours tick by. It's getting harder to breathe with each step. You are competing head-on with the elements. It's amazing that each step now actually makes a noticeable difference in your breathing. You're certainly working harder – and for the first time in your journey, it's now a struggle.

You're surprised that even with all of your training and intensive preparation your footing is becoming less sure. You're definitely in uncharted territory here. Time to dig deep. You're not able to think quite as clearly as you'd like; things appear less familiar and you are somewhat disoriented. Perhaps it's the elevation; this is clearly threatening territory. You're fighting off the elements and the surrounding conditions. You find that your decisions are taking a little longer to make. And they're somewhat compromised because you're short an essential ingredient to your survival - oxygen. Unphased, you keep marching on. Onward and upward. Just keep on going. Keep doing what you're doing. It has gotten you this far, hasn't it?

As you muster your persistence and all of your reserves to keep climbing, you notice that you're starting to make mistakes. Just small ones at first. You left your gloves off just a little too long while you were checking your instruments. You can recover from that, it's OK. Then you strayed just a tad from the main trail, no big deal. Yet it did cost energy and oxygen; precious oxygen which is in increasingly short supply up here. Now you are back on track, back on the path to the summit. At this stage, it's beginning to sink in that this is much harder than you thought it would be. Even with all of the preparation, you didn't expect the struggle to be quite this intense. Brute force can only take you so far up the mountain. You need to keep your wits about you and make better decisions. You need to avoid costly mistakes. Now your very survival is at stake. Mistakes at this altitude can cost you more than you want to think about.

Another hour goes by. Almost unimaginably, it's colder and the air is thinner. And the wind is howling remorselessly. Yet the white peak beckons, the summit is in sight. But seeing the summit is very different from reaching it. Thinking it is far from achieving it. The massive effort that it took to get you to where you are has come with a big cost; it has drained everything out of you. Now you're simply floundering about what to do next. You have everything on the line, you're all in. You're thinking: If I just keep moving forward, place one foot in front of the other. If I just keep doing what I'm doing, then everything will be OK. Isn't that the way you planned and prepared? You will meet your goal; you will reach the top of the mountain. Hard work and solid effort will win the day.

Isn't that the winning formula?

Maybe that's true in the gym, but not on the mountain or in your business. Many business owners are working harder and harder but they're not making the progress they expect. Sheer effort alone is not going to get the job done to reach their Peak Profit Potential. It's going to take more oxygen ..... which in your business is information, management information. It's essential for your business survival. It's essential for your business to grow. Without it, you could simply be wasting your time and your money. Your business is going nowhere. Information is the lifeblood of your business. Just like oxygen on the mountain, you need all of the essentials to make good decisions in your business. Doing more of the same will only get you more of the same...or worse.

> ... *management information* is the oxygen in your business.....

How do you discover the essential elements you need to succeed? If running your business has left you exhausted and wondering what to do next, it could be the lack of critical management information that is holding you back. That is keeping you stuck. This knowledge gap is jeopardizing the very survival of your business. Running your business without essential information is a risky play indeed.

Next we will explore cost drivers and the impact they have on your business.

Cost Drivers

Costs are associated with each activity in your business; your major business processes define your most important cost drivers. Cost drivers can cause both expected and unexpected changes in the cost of an activity. Sometimes they are straightforward such as paper in a print shop; it's easy to see the linear relationship. In other cases, costs can jump if you exceed the limits of a machine and require maintenance, repairs, or undue wear and tear which could shorten the useful life of an asset. A hidden cost in many businesses is rework, is that true for your business?

The fact is the main difference between marginally profitable companies and highly profitable ones is that highly profitable ones control their costs better. Yes, these companies still make investments; they still

> *... highly profitable companies **control their costs** better.*

spend money. They aggressively pursue growth opportunities. The difference is that they never lose sight of their cost drivers. They're not interested in increasing their profits linearly; they're looking for exponential growth in profits through economies of scale. If your costs are moving up in lock step with your volume, then you're on a treadmill. Your business does not scale in terms of profitability, so increased business always means increased work; it will never get easier.

Take a closer look at your costs, how they behave, and why. It's time to bring your costs in line with your profit margin targets. If you have economies of scale, each new unit should cost less to produce. Increasing volumes help to spread your fixed costs. And there also might be significant opportunities when looking at your variable costs. Shipping two books is generally not twice as expensive as shipping one.

As you proceed, recognize that most activities have more than one cost driver. Think of land, labor, and capital then add in materials, supplies, utilities, and other costs. Select an important process in your business and begin to identify your relevant cost drivers. There may be more than you first realized. After you master one area, move on to identify cost drivers in other areas of your business in priority order.

Value Drivers

Relative customer value is accrued along the value chain in your business; these are value drivers. Taken collectively, customer value assessments help to reduce the common flaw of nearsightedness when making decisions only based on a single, yet significant, business process. The new mission for your business could be: Drive for high quality and high speed to provide outstanding customer value at a higher profit. That's what successful and profitable businesses do.

There are two dimensions of value in your business: value to the customer and value to your business. In many cases they are fully aligned yet many things that you need to do in your business impact your clients indirectly or not at all. Paying taxes is one example.

Know the Value of Your Time

One of the biggest value drivers in your business is, not unexpectedly, you. There may have been times in your business when you thought: I need another me! That is a common refrain among those working in small businesses. After all, your primary value is your time and expertise. There is only one of you and you can only be in one place doing one thing at a time. Even for those who consider themselves to be highly successful at multitasking, the truth is that your brain is really only doing one thing at a time; as it switches from thought to thought you lose efficiency and context while you increase your stress levels. Not the best path for Peak Profit Potential.

It's important to know the value of an hour of your time at its best usage. We'll explore two levels of time analysis that are relevant for your business: strategic and operational. At the strategic level your activities include reaching out and reaching up to the marketplace and external parties. Some of the strategic activities are listed in the chart.

Strategic Uses of Your Time

✔ Formulating the business strategy
✔ Securing financing
✔ Coordinating investor relations
✔ Planning
✔ Selecting target markets
✔ Identifying the offerings
✔ Designing the marketing approach
✔ Developing a sales strategy
✔ Networking
✔ Managing communications

Each of these strategic activities needs to be done. You can decide whether they are to be done by you or by someone else. Each of these activities provides value to your business. Each of these activities also has a cost. As you assess your role in the strategic activities of your business, compare the cost of an hour of your time with the value generated by that hour. The CEO as chief strategist can be valued at more than $500 per hour. Not all business owners and managers are good at each of these and other strategic tasks. Your business could be accruing the costs without reaping the expected benefits and capturing the value of the hour. Where you have the skills and competencies, work these activities into your schedule when it makes sense. Where you don't, get the help you need and focus your time on higher-value activities.

At the operational level your activities are wide ranging; sample operational activities are listed in the chart.

Operational Uses of Your Time

✔ Selling new work
✔ Coordinating pricing decisions
✔ Scheduling and completing work
✔ Prioritizing resource utilization
✔ Evaluating the offerings in use
✔ Enforcing customer service policies
✔ Managing payables and receivables
✔ Overseeing quality and standards
✔ Communicating work programs

Each of these and many more operational activities needs to be done. Once again, you decide whether you or someone else is doing them. Each of these activities has both a value and a cost. As you assess your role in the operational activities of your business, compare the cost of an hour of your time with the value generated by that hour of your time. Just like in the strategic tasks, not all business owners and managers are good at each of these tasks. Where you have the skills and competencies, work these activities into your schedule when it makes sense. Where you don't, delegate them to enable you to focus on higher-value activities.

The Drive for Value

The key question to explore regarding how to value your time is: What is the best use of your time right now? What can you be doing right now that has the highest value in terms of planning for the future, increasing revenues, increasing profits, or reducing excess costs? Each hour of every day the answer will be different. Thinking and planning are essential business activities. Be relentless. What is the best use of your time after you read this book today?

Given the volume of work that you are currently delivering, how well are you blending management, sales, and admin activities into your week? Your month? You can take advantage of the principle of the highest value of your time even when fully booked. Interleaving client work with running your business is a critical success factor. And as contracts run their course, selling your next jobs while you are busy with your current jobs is an important dimension of sustained profitability. Take the long-term view regarding the best use of your time. The idea is to maximize revenues while at the same time effectively managing your business. There are always marketing, administrative, and other activities that need to be completed no matter what. And then there is the dream about you having a life outside of your business. And fun. Yes, fun.

Even if you do not bill out your time by the hour directly to your customers, your hour has a billable value. It is the value of the highest use of your time at any given juncture. Think about what you contribute as the CEO of the operation. That is the value of your hour until all of the critical CEO tasks are completed. Then move to the next most important activity; perhaps it is sales. If you're good at sales, your hour has a high value linked directly to new revenues. If you're not, it's time to think about hiring professional sales people or using partners.

Work down the list; these and other activities come into consideration as immediate business issues are resolved. These activities can include business strategy, marketing, networking, customer interaction, invoicing, collections, system development, and identifying resources. At each stage in your business these activities play a large role in adding value to your business; many add value directly to the customer. Each hour of your time has an intrinsic value. Your mission is to devote your time to the most valuable strategic or operational activity and then move down the list maintaining an effective balance over the longer term even if some weeks are a little crazy and out of control.

Think Value All Day Long

One recommendation from time management specialists is to spend the first 15 to 30 minutes at the beginning of the day analyzing what is the most important thing for you to be doing. After that, get to work. It is better to get the tough tasks behind you early in the day. Let's face it. The work is not going away. It simply needs to be done. By you. Completing a difficult task early in the day gives you a sense of accomplishment. Then your outlook for the rest of the day is much brighter.

As you plan your day carve out time blocks that I call **profit slots**, such as 30 to 90 minutes to complete each task while you're in the flow without interruptions. At the end of two hours, take a short break. Come back and begin again with your profit slots as planned in the morning. After lunch, repeat the same process: analyze what is the most important thing for you to be doing right now. Plan the rest of your afternoon accordingly. At the end of the day you will be amazed that the simple technique of blocking time in profit slots in the morning and allocating time to the highest value activity is extremely powerful and strategic. It does take discipline to make it work, but it's well worth it. This is a valuable habit that will serve you well throughout your business career.

Time Wasters are Value Killers

How much time do you waste on the phone? You can put an end to insidious phone tag for good by having a comprehensive phone strategy in place. Many people are busy and it can take three or four tries to actually connect. So consider text, voicemail, e-mail, or any other mode when you're asking a specific question and need a specific answer. If you need a two-way conversation, schedule the call. Busy professionals respect the time of others as well as their own.

Another huge time waster in small business is email. We are flooded with it every day; it has truly become a costly nuisance. Millions of emails messages per day yet half of it is spam! How can you receive your essential messages without all of the noise?

One simple way is to have your email screened before you look at it. Another way is to direct it to your website where it can be categorized with drop-down menus and then monitored. Getting mail out of your inbox altogether helps to avoid spam and time wasters. Then there is the internet. The problem is the ratio of productive time to unproductive time on the internet is quite low. We tend to linger long after we found what we were originally looking for. The internet is in the top three time wasters in many small businesses. The power of search, news, and videos is overwhelming; we all seem to fall under the spell. (I won't even mention the cat videos.) Plan your internet time in advance and stick to your schedule. Craft an internet research strategy similar to your phone strategy to preserve your valuable time.

Customer Value Planning

In *Ready, Fire, Aim* author Michael Masterson states that the secret to breaking into new markets is to create tipping points by finding hot products in rising markets and finding some way to make them new and different. Along the same lines, Mike Koenigs believes that there are five questions you should be asking related to providing unequaled customer value.

✔ Who am I selling to?
✔ What problem can I solve for them?
✔ What will get them to buy from me?
✔ How do I position my product and my business for maximum revenue?
✔ How can I help my customers make more money?

Many master marketers advocate that you have a logical progression of offerings that your customers would like to buy. They might be interested in buying more advanced and more expensive items from you over time as they grow. Plan to be there when they need you. Never stop thinking about increasing customer value. It's all about them. According to Jay Abraham, your goal is to surpass all others by providing added value and empathetic connection; these sources of earned trust will ultimately compel people to pay you a premium price for your product. Of course, there is also the strategy to sell only premium products and services right out of the gate.

Look closely at your current business processes in the context of customer value. Assess how every major step of the way builds customer value, from their perspective, not yours. Look at process consistency and replicability; how do these attributes

> *… excess variability without adding customer value is a surefire quality and **profit killer**.*

increase customer value? How do you know? Excess process variability without adding equivalent customer value is a surefire quality and profit killer. Explore why there is variability in products or processes in the first place: people, tools, timing, technique, materials, complexity, and individual customer requests can all influence your process and product variability. Knowing how specific aspects of process variability, desirable or otherwise, drive additional costs and contribute to or reduce customer value is important to fully understanding what to change and what to charge in your business. Ask your customers what they value; you just might be way off base with your assumptions. (For an interesting audio on value drivers, go to *www.PeakProfitPotential.com/valuedrivers.*)

Profit Drivers

There are elements of your business that are proceeding exceedingly well. These have helped drive your profits in the past. Designing a suite of offerings that meet or exceed your customers' needs is the essential activity of your business. Yet how that value is delivered to each customer separates profitable businesses from unprofitable ones. It takes productivity…. strategic productivity. Managing to achieve strategic productivity is a critical success factor in every business, and yours is no different. It's doing the right things right. An eye on detail reveals all along the way what can be done better, cheaper, faster, or at higher quality. Perhaps one way to bundle your outbound orders cuts down on cycle time by 20%. Finding better materials offered at an 11% discount not only increases durability but also customer value. Every step along the way, all of your inputs and processes can be optimized and balanced as profit drivers.

According to Brian Tracy, 84% of all sales in America originate from recommendations by a satisfied customer. A new customer referral is worth ten times more than a cold call. And it's 16 times easier to sell a satisfied customer something new than it is to sell to a new prospect. What steps can you take now to dramatically increase customer satisfaction and thus drive profits? These are your profit drivers.

In some cases after-sales service is the main reason some customers buy from you. And when you know that, your marketing materials can feature that aspect prominently. Differentiation for differentiation's sake is wasted effort. Yet the constant search for new and innovative ways to increase profits, while at the same time monitoring cost and value drivers, is the way to have an outstanding business.

Putting It All Together

If you are so busy each day that you spend all of your time heads down delivering work, you may be missing strategic opportunities to boost profitability and grow your business. If you're in a constant rush, then perhaps a

> ... Differentiation for differentiation's sake is a wasted effort...

weekly plan might work best for you. If you're currently crunching on an important project or deliverable, get that out the door, and then begin your plan with your full concentration. But mark that planning time on your calendar now; the time slot will not stay open for long.

If it makes more sense based on your current workload, begin with a monthly appointment so that essential business planning activities are booked into your schedule and are not left to chance. You'll be surprised at what just 30 minutes of uninterrupted planning time could do for your business in terms of identifying new markets, new customers, new partners, and new processes. And most professionals find it to be fun. As you gain more control over your time, the target is to spend at least 60 minutes per week, every week.

It's important to be realistic as you begin. Build in any expected and unexpected delays into your time planning each week. The plan has to work for you in your business or else it will go on the scrap heap like all of the plans that came before it. This time is different. This time you are on the right track. This time it will work. The best time forecast is only as good as your best assumptions. What are your current time pressures and challenges? Who is making demands on your time? How much time are you spending with customers? What activities are important for you to do vs. what can be done by others? Think about making some changes so that you don't extrapolate the past on to the future and get more of the same.

Key Questions in Your Time Value Assessment

- ✔ What is the value of one hour of your time?
- ✔ What is the cost of one hour of your time?
- ✔ What activities are absolutely necessary for you to do yourself?
- ✔ What activities can be eliminated entirely?
- ✔ What activities can be completed by someone else, including the client?
- ✔ What is the second most valuable use of your time?
- ✔ What is the third most valuable use of your time?
- ✔ Are you billing enough to cover your support staff? Overhead?
- ✔ When will you complete your time value analysis?
- ✔ What information do you need to improve the accuracy of your analysis?

The impact of your business process review to identify significant cost, value, and profit drivers can vary directly with the risks you're willing to take to make changes, if you believe that maintaining the status quo is risk free. Many business owners believe that sitting still is a no-risk option. Nothing can be further from the truth. Just think about the newspaper industry and the recent shifts; the world has changed and will continue to change at an accelerated pace. What will the news industry look like in three years?

Traditional Risk and Impact Grid

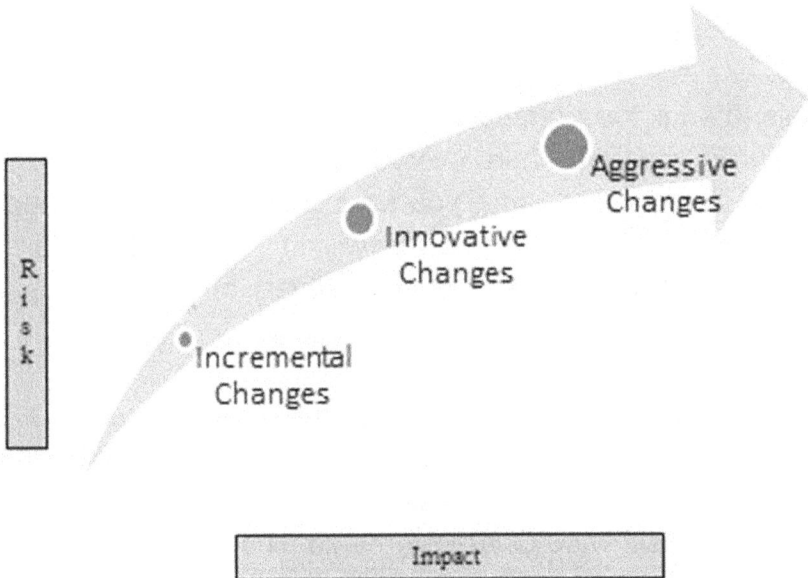

Your strategic attention, looking up and out from your business and looking toward the future, defines the big picture of your business. It defines the ways in which your business will look similar three years from now and the ways in which it will look distinctly different. Aggressive changes often carry a bigger risk yet can have a greater impact when carried out well. The ultimate test is whether the proposed changes or innovations build customer value. Your operational attention, looking inside your business, defines the processes at work today. Incremental changes can be implemented in the normal course of business and also through focused profit improvement initiatives. Blending both the big picture strategic view with the day-to-day operational view enables you to keep your eye on the ball while swinging for the fences.

Every business is different and their risks and drivers are different. Every business starts from a different place. Only you know your business. Only you know current commitments and what else is on your plate right now. Beware of setting unrealistic goals. It's far too common. Perhaps you've gone to a seminar and while you were there everything sounded great. You were fully on board. At the time, you were convinced that you needed to take action. You were not only willing to act, but also excited to act. You were ready to implement every one of the ideas that you heard. So, what happened?

When you got back home, you realized that you were already overbooked; actually you discovered that you had negative free time. There were so many pressing issues, and even some emergencies to deal with. Gradually the seminar high began to fade and you found yourself right back where you started. I know how you feel; I've done it myself - and more than once. Only now you are a bit more frustrated because you thought that attending the seminar was actually going to make things better in your business right away. Just like the brochure said, right? But follow up was absent or much less than was needed.

The point is that you have now embarked upon a business performance management journey of continuous performance measurement and action. Minus the hotel and the airfare. You can't unknow what you now know. You can't go back to the time when you didn't realize the incredible power of cost drivers, value drivers, and profit drivers to streamline your business processes, to increase customer value, and to boost your profits. Now you know. And you will never look at your business the same way again. And that's a good thing.

Moving Forward

The goal is to set a realistic plan that will work in your business with your schedule given everything else that you've got going on. You're already mega-busy so take care in making your plan. I really want you to experience the incredible power of these tools. I really want you to succeed. The only way that's going to happen is if you're realistic.

Many small business owners choose an incremental approach to dip a toe in the business performance management and business intelligence waters. You too can start with low-risk incremental business process changes just to see what you uncover. Or you can be more adventurous and roll out a new product or a whole new way of doing things. You can be very aggressive and decide to advance your entire business strategy. There is no one right answer for you and your business. It's all up to you. What are you ready for right here, right now? The most important message is to take action now. Make this the time when you fully implement the tools with a solid commitment to success.

SWOT Analysis

As you begin to explore business performance measures and enhance your decision making tools, a SWOT analysis is

> *... Many small business owners choose **an incremental approach**...*

helpful to explore your Strengths, Weaknesses, Opportunities, and Threats. This analysis can help you to assess potential threats and opportunities for your business that generally are not top-of-mind. A sample SWOT analysis presents a few internal strengths and weaknesses and external opportunities and threats.

Sample Areas for SWOT Analysis

Internal	Strengths	Weaknesses
	New product pipeline	Aging products
	Streamlined processes	High fixed costs
	Skilled team	Unclear strategy
	Solid systems	Expensive rework
External	Opportunities	Threats
	Partners	Competitors
	Innovation	Recession
	New markets	Falling demand
	New supply chains	Financing gaps

When you're ready to do your own SWOT analysis, a sample worksheet for you to complete the analysis of your business can be found at *www.PeakProfitPotential.com/swot*. Candidly assess the internal strengths and weaknesses of your business. Explore the external opportunities and threats to your business. Take your time and get creative with this. It's not often that you take the time to sit down and think about both the internal elements as well as the external factors facing your business at the same time. Bring both your strategic attention and your operational attention to the table. Use this sample list as an idea generator to get you started then make it your own.

Think of ways in which your SWOT analysis would be somewhat similar to the sample and ways that yours would be quite different. As a note of experience, it can be quite revealing as well as empowering to put the threats to your business in writing. Once revealed, these threats are fair game to be conquered in your business strategy, market positioning, cost profile, and every facet of your business. The proactive manager, the informed manager makes strategic decisions to identify a few areas to focus on first to analyze, collect the data, and take action.

Business Owner as Risk Manager

With performance management tools at your disposal, you can face business risks head on. Why not master them and use them to your advantage? Think of ways in which your SWOT analysis can inform your business strategy.

SWOT → Strategy → Design → Implement → Measure

As your business strategy evolves, the next step is to design or redesign business processes that will effectively deliver on that strategy. As the designs are perfected, they move to careful implementation. This is where the rubber meets the road, and it may require that you modify the designs slightly or significantly to get it right. Resist the temptation to cut corners on business process implementation. The last step is to measure for results. Effective performance measurement is repetitive loop in an environmentally scanning, sensing, breathing business. It reflects a dynamic world in which dynamic businesses claim more than their fair share of profits. Sometimes it's difficult to quantify risks and to estimate potential rewards. You know your business and your markets better than anyone. But when going into uncharted territory look for those in the know such as an industry leader, a mentor, a trusted advisor, or a supplier. Use the available data. Use and test a few performance measures. Roll in a few trusted expert opinions. Then use your judgment to decide where you will take action first.

In carrying out this process only risk what is reasonable; go for hitting a reliable single unless you have the financial backing to go for a home run with shared risk and reward scenarios. Cut excess costs. Streamline operations. Add new product and service extensions. Add new types of customers. Use new marketing channels. Any business decision that is supported by accurate data to increase customer value can be augmented with effective performance measures.

CHAPTER 4

BUSINESS PERFORMANCE MANAGEMENT

You are surrounded by simple, obvious solutions that can dra-
matically increase your income, power, influence and success.
The problem is you just don't see them. Jay Abraham

Business performance management means different things to
different people and it can be applied to different processes
within your business. According to Dr. Aubrey Daniels, performance management includes activities which ensure that goals
are consistently being met in an effective and efficient manner.
Performance management can focus on the organization, a department, or process to build a product or service, as well as
many other areas. Business performance management is also
known as a process by which organizations align their resources,
systems, and teams with strategic objectives and priorities.

The emphasis on managing organizational performance has
been around for years and supports the achievement of both
strategic and operational goals. In *Integrating Strategy Execution,*
Methodologies, Risk, and Analytics[1], Gary Cokins pulls it all together and reminds us that what gets measured gets done. And

---

1 *Performance Management - Integrating Strategy Execution, Methodologies,*
Risk, and Analytics. Gary Cokins, John Wiley & Sons, Inc. 2009. ISBN
978-0-470-44998-1

The Balanced Scorecard created by Kaplan and Norton[2] has been widely used in large corporations. Yet business performance management need not be overly complex to give you the results you're looking for in your business. Businesses of all sizes can benefit greatly from well-designed performance management activities.

The benefits of proactive performance management reach across your company and can include every measure in your business. At certain times, some are more important than others. Yet they combine to form the basis of solid business intelligence at your fingertips.

What Performance Management Can Do For Your Business

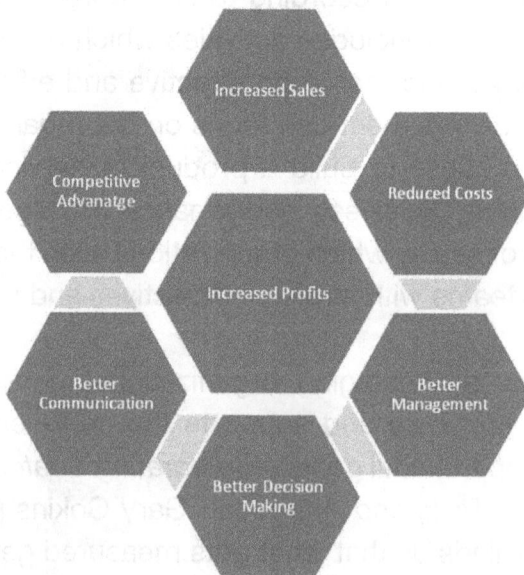

Increased Sales

Competitive Advantage

Reduced Costs

Increased Profits

Better Communication

Better Management

Better Decision Making

---

2 *The Balanced Scorecard: Translating Strategy into Action,* Harvard Business School Press, Boston (1996)

Multiple Roles of Business Performance Management

As the owner of your business you play many roles. Chief Executive Officer (CEO) is the natural first role that many in small business fully claim. It's your business and as the leader you make the executive decisions. You call the shots so the CEO moniker is appropriate. You are in charge of and responsible for ...everything.

Not far behind that role is Chief Financial Officer (CFO) who as well plays a major role in many important areas of the business. In large corporations, CFO roles can include:

✔ Capital & Funding
✔ Tax & Compliance
✔ Planning & Budgeting
✔ Operations & Costing
✔ Performance Management

As the CFO of a small business, you fulfill the same roles; it's simply a matter of scale. Whereas the Fortune 500 CFO approaches Wall Street for capital, the small business owner works with banks, investors, sponsors, venture capitalists, and other sources to secure needed funds for the business. Whereas the Fortune 500 CFO manages Wall Street's quarterly expectations, the small business owner generally manages toward annual targets and loan terms. Whereas the Fortune 500 CFO manages performance for senior management and stockholders, small business owners manage performance for their livelihoods and their creditors.

In the CFO role your job is to analyze, understand, manage, and mitigate processes that drive cash through the business. Tracking cash through the business value chain connects purchasing to payables to drive excess costs down, and quality and timeliness up. In the same vein, linking product delivery to receivables management delivers profits to the bottom line. While generating profits keeps you in business over the long term, cash is the life blood in all businesses. Ready cash flow is a powerful indicator of the health of your business. Cash provides a window into the interlocking gears of your business. Where are the cash pinch points in your business and what do they mean? How do they affect your business performance?

Business Process Analysis

In cases where there is either a shortage or backlog of orders, the conditions are completely different when compared to the case where orders are flowing smoothly through your business. An insightful analysis will assess whether every step in your process creates customer value. Every step takes time and resources so it's important that every step adds customer value and thus, contributes to cash flow. Rework is the bane of profitability. It can boost costs and delay cash collections. Everything that you can do to do things right the first time can pay off big time as it carries through to:

Quality

Cycle Time

Customer Satisfaction

Be relentless in the pursuit of quality. It separates you from all the other players in the marketplace. Quality lasts. Quality impresses. Quality builds customer loyalty and referrals. Speed only plays a role after the quality parameters are fully in place. Imagine taking your car in to have it professionally detailed; you can almost see the sparkle and shine. The tires are jet black and unbelievable. You were hoping for the "A" team because they always do a great job on your car. But you'll have to wait 30 minutes for the "A" team. Or else you can have the "B" team work on your car right away, but you have no idea about the quality of their work. What is the better deal? In more than 90% of the cases, quality wins out. You'll wait for the "A" team. The same desire for uncompromising quality also applies to your customers. (For an interesting audio on the relationship between quality and cost, go to *www. PeakProfitPotential.com/quality*.)

Having your team, your resources, and your capital equipment fully directed toward generating customer value and customer satisfaction is the way to transform your business. After all, you are the "A" team, aren't you? Quality drives profits and brings in cash. It's not about simply being busy. It's about effectively directing resources in an optimal way to produce quality and customer value which leads to cash. It can mean all hands on deck when a product is almost complete. I remember from my early consulting days when we had to assemble 100 binders with every sort of odd-sized document you could ever imagine. It was all-hands-on-deck in a huge conference room where partners, directors, managers, consultants, and admins alike were all stuffing inserts into those binders to get the job done on time and at high quality. The binders were directly linked to client value and thus, directly linked to cash. Now, was this a standard practice in an international consulting firm? Absolutely not! Does it work when you need it to? Absolutely yes!

The overriding message is:

✔ Immediate Value Creation Informs Current Priorities
✔ Long-term Value Creation informs Strategic Priorities
✔ Blend Both to Build Sustainable Customer Value

Processes that build value are essential in a sustainable business. Processes that build value that are predictable, repeatable, and reliable are the hallmarks of a profitable business. Linking customer service to cash is a solid technique not only when delivering your products but also when reformulating or expanding them. The primary question is: Does any proposed change bring increased value to the customer that they are willing to pay for? That is business performance management in action.

As CFO, one of your primary roles is the persistent pursuit of value. Do your current performance measures consistently build or kill value in your business? How do you know? The goal is to use numbers that mean something related to your business performance. Numbers will show you whether your business strategy is or isn't working. Getting your excess costs under control is the first step. That sets your business up for profitable growth. It's folly to expand even as you are leaking profits. Identify and cut excess costs and then your business can expand on a lower-cost platform to yield exponential profits.

Results in your bottom line can tell you whether what you're doing overall is working, plain and simple. Yet without the underlying details provided by business performance management systems, some products might be major contributors to profit while, at the same time, other products could be eroding profits. Shared understanding across your business and across your team is an important dimension of meeting your performance targets; having everyone rowing the boat in the same direction is vital. Tracking your costs to acquire a customer then serving your customers well with high quality products is essential in every dimension of your business. Taking care of your customers while watching your costs is a key factor in managing the profit equation of your business.

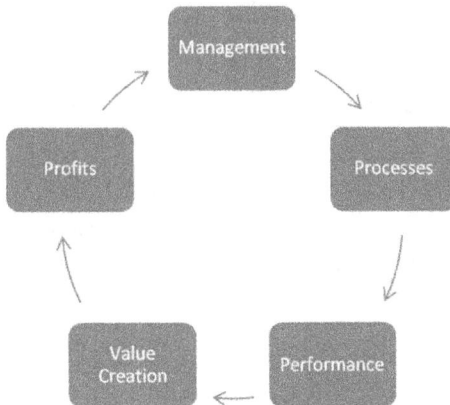

A business performance management and value creation mindset is effective both in good times and in bad. When your sales are high, there is time for innovation. When your sales are a little slow, there is increased urgency. Performance management can be driven by internal factors, external factors, or both. In any case, the objective is to monitor and measure business activities against results. Management drives processes. Performance drives customer value. Value drives profits. This is a powerful way of thinking; it puts you back in charge of your business, back in the driver's seat. Performance management fully embodies the essential characteristics of business leadership. (For an audio on the Performance Management Mindset, go to *www. PeakProfitPotential.com/mindset*.)

Customer Value Lens

From now on, look at every major business decision you make through a new lens – a customer value lens. If you continue to provide increasing levels of value to your customers that they're willing to pay for, and you do it with integrity, your profits will increase. And as a result, you will gain market share. In effect, you will be building higher walls around your business by innovating in areas that directly drive customer value. Warren Buffett only invests in companies that successfully create a moat around their businesses to block competitors. When you start building extreme value in your business, your customers will begin to notice and your profits will begin to rise.

Customer value comes in all shapes and sizes including: unique features, reliability, risk management, persistent adherence to specifications, timeliness, consistency, affordability, convenience, and providing value to your customers' customers. Basically, value is what your customers define it to be, so ask them. Take the time to get to know their business needs. Identify the major pinch points in their businesses as they relate to your offerings. Look for gaps in their processes that slow them down or cost them money and identify where your products might assist.

The goal is to move away from competing on price, as far away as possible. You offer a unique package of customer value that is like no other, right? It's important to have competitive pricing, but not to compete in the lowest price race to the bottom. Commodity markets are best left to the pros. You want an undisputed competitive advantage for your business. You want an advantage that is sustainable. If you don't have one, now is the time to create one.

As you can see, value creation drives what successful businesses do. Just as important, it drives what they don't do. Take a look at the myriad of activities that you're doing every day in your business. Step back and take a cold, hard look at where you and your team spend most of your time. You might be quite surprised at the huge amount of time spent on low-value activities. Just because you've always done something doesn't mean that it's immune from the value creation test. To review, the best way to find out what customers specifically value about your business is to ask them. What you assume they think is important might not be, and vice versa. This exercise can be a real eye opener for small business owners. After reaching out to their customers, many businesses adopt a whole new strategic focus based on frank, detailed customer feedback.

Innovate with Care

One way to build customer value is through innovation. Successful innovation drives business success and builds more of a moat around your business. That means there will be some failures; they are to be expected. Under closer inspection, many shiny new opportunities begin to fade and lose their luster. In many cases, they cannot deliver on their promise to create additional customer value. Oftentimes, initial expectations were far too high to begin with. Yet in countless other cases, these forays into uncharted territory can lead to a valuable business idea realized by adapting products based on continuous market feedback.

Innovations that align with or extend what you're already doing pose the lowest risk and have a higher likelihood of payoff. If you've got an idea that's not closely aligned with your current business, research it carefully based on an analysis of your competitive advantage, your marketplace, your resources, and your knowledge, skills, and experience. Many companies allocate a set percentage of time and funds for innovation and research to keep them out in front as a provider of solutions to consistently meet customer needs.

The Power of "What"

Just as a 4-year old repeatedly asks "why, why, why" to almost everything you say, the relentless value seeker asks "what" to every activity. These four questions shine a light on what's important to your customers.

- ✔ What is the value to the customer?
- ✔ What features will customers gladly pay for?
- ✔ What is the reason to buy from only you?
- ✔ What is the profit contribution of this activity?

Knowing "what" helps to guide performance measures in your business. When you add new performance measures, discard old ones that are no longer serving you. Tracking the wrong performance measures is perilous. Having too many measures is worse than having too few. With too many, you might actually think that you've got good, actionable information to drive value in your business. Nothing could be further from the truth. 72% of CFOs surveyed said they have too many measures pulling the business in too many different directions. Learn from the big boys' mistakes and keep performance management simple in your business. Tracking irrelevant measures could be costing you valuable time and money which is really ironic because you are tracking them solely to improve your business.

If you're not ready to overhaul all of your performance measures right now, then when you formulate a new measure, delete one. You want to avoid having too many measures without generating commensurate value. When it comes to business performance measures, less is definitely more.

On the other hand, if you can take the time now, wipe the slate clean of all of your performance measures and begin anew. Make each measure or indicator prove its worth in your new value creation mindset. Make each measure drive customer value and profits in your business.

Test, Test, and Retest

When new measures are put in place, the next step is to test them. Test, test, and retest. Take the time to get them right before you fully operationalize performance measures in your business. It's a common failing to develop a very nice set of indicators on paper only to have them fall down on testing, implementing, and tracking. The proof is:

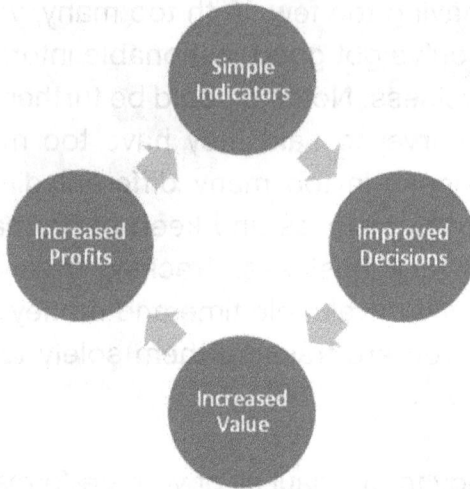

Increasing profits in your business; that's the goal. The right indicators can improve your decision making. Better decisions lead to increased customer value. Value drives profits. The hidden feature of this is that the value creation formula that drives profits can be applied at multiple levels in your business, again and again.

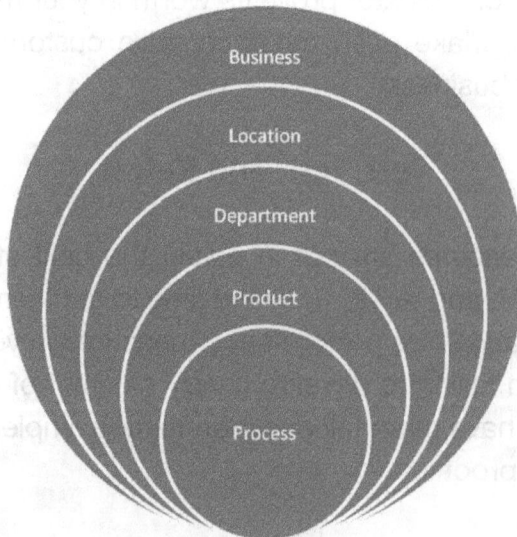

At each level, the analytical process is the same yet the language of value is quite different. Take a look at a specific process. The people actually performing a process know it inside and out. They know what's working and what's not. And they probably have ideas as to how to improve operational business processes. Those looking in from the outside only have a partial understanding, an incomplete perception. Go directly to the source for the best information and deeper understanding. This also works at every other level in your business such as product or service offerings, departments and divisions, facilities and locations, as well as the overall business.

Performance Management Case Study

Calvin runs an e-learning company that creates on-line training modules to simplify new medical instrumentation systems for users. Calvin as CEO is outward looking with an eye toward expanding to new markets and bringing in new customers. The CFO is looking outward for pricing direction and inward for costing information. The actual product creators are developing individual training software in modules. Customer value means different things to each of these actors in their respective roles. The design process to map out the training modules and link them logically together to achieve the leaning objectives is performed by the e-learning program creator. His view of customer value lies in the user interface, the graphic representations, sound, and tying the comprehension testing directly back to the content. So comprehension and ease of use are his value drivers.

Therefore, measures to drive down the number of modules to a minimum or reduce the number of screens in each module to cut costs could be hugely counterproductive to the learning objectives and thus, to customer value. Each member of the team can communicate their diverse viewpoints using their own language under the organizing framework of customer value. Veering too far in one direction with unsuitable performance measures will take Calvin's company away from its stated goals. In many cases, a more balanced view of increasing customer value is what's needed to boost business profits.

Your Business Context

Profits are the key to your business being in a whole new league three years from now. When running your small business you receive feedback continuously from suppliers and customers as well as from partners, staff, and others. Often there is so much feedback sometimes it's difficult to synthesize or prioritize. What does it all mean? How does it all fit together, if at all? And what is the most important message? When the messages relate to small business profits and your overall profitability, they take on added significance.

Sound decision making is based on weighing the relevant evidence and available data, placing it in the proper context for your business, then choosing from a viable set of alternative courses of action. After a decision is reached, it is implemented and then tracked to measure the actual impact against the planned results. This creates a self-reinforcing feedback loop where outcomes are objectively assessed against plans. Most performance measures are not perfect right out of the gate. When used with a constructive mindset, variance analysis noting what happened vs. what was expected is not a blame game rather it's a direct path to profit gain.

When you manage by exception you focus a very valuable and scare resource, your attention. This focus enables you to guide your attention toward significant areas in your business where variances from plans have occurred. Little of your operational attention is needed on areas that are going well; focus instead on resolving the pressing issues at hand. When the boat is leaking, the first order of business is to patch and bail. Leaky boats don't stay afloat for long. Later your strategic attention can explore areas that are working well yet could still be improved during your weekly innovation and brain storming time.

Keep It Simple

An underlying principle for performance management to support decision making in small business is simplicity. Get the information you need and only what you need. Adding unwarranted complexity merely adds costs without a commensurate value; a non-starter. Another way to look at this: Systems that track exceptions can be classified in two ways, by providing either ongoing mainstream business information or special one-off analytical information. Mainstream information systems warrant judicious investments of capital, time, training, and controls. In contrast, one-off analyses of non-recurring decisions including pricing, order acceptance, make or buy, or outsourcing are likely supported more cost effectively using a spreadsheet or other simple business analyses. The idea is to have the critical information you need at your fingertips when you need it – in a cost-effective manner.

> ... *focus enables you to **guide your attention** toward significant areas in your business.*

CHAPTER 5

THE PROFIT PYRAMID™

Customers today want the very most and the very best
for the very least amount of money, and on the best terms.
Only the individuals and companies that provide absolutely
excellent products and services at absolutely excellent
prices will survive. Brian Tracy

Across businesses of all sizes, better measurement results in better management. You just have to know where to begin. There are different types of measures for different industries but many share the same common themes: operational, financial, and administrative. There are also many different sources for measures: Are they externally focused on customers, suppliers, creditors, or others? Or are they internally focused on processes, efficiency, quality, or other dimensions? Whatever measures you've been using up until now can be reevaluated in order to identify what's emerging as important going forward.

Even though many measures track data from the past, they can also be forward looking and predictive in nature and intention. Each performance measure at every level should support, and not undermine, your overall business strategy, as in the hospital example presented earlier. Delivering the highest customer value while maximizing profits is your overarching business objective.

It's time to look at your business, including your business strategy. It forms the foundation in The Profit Pyramid™ supporting the other six elements.

The Profit Pyramid™

The seven dimensions of The Profit Pyramid™ cover a wide array of performance management issues in your business. A brief description of each of these dimensions is provided below:

- ✔ **Profit** – revenues minus costs in running your business
- ✔ **Value** - tangible and intangible benefits received and acknowledged by your customers
- ✔ **Results** – outcomes achieved based on inputs and outputs
- ✔ **Measures** – concrete and quantitative ways to assess goal completion
- ✔ **Goals** – specific, measurable targets accompanied by dates for achievement

> ✔ **Objectives** –how to serve your customers in fulfilling the mission of your business
> ✔ **Strategy** – how your business delivers value, in what forms, and to which customers.

Four Key Questions

It is not news that when running your business, there are many demands on your time. Today's business owners are looking for ways to make their lives easier and for creative ways to free up their most important resource, their time. One way to cut through the clutter is to apply The Profit Pyramid™ to your business. Start out at a very high level across all seven dimensions and use it as a diagnostic to identify fertile areas where you can drill down for a more in-depth analysis. Go to *www.PeakProfitPotential.com/ pyramid* for a helpful worksheet to get you started. After you complete the overview level of The Profit Pyramid™, select one area to concentrate on for the next phase of your analysis. Here are four key questions for you to consider:

> ✔ How is my business doing now on each of these seven dimensions?
> ✔ How does my business performance compare to plan?
> ✔ Are the key trends moving in the right direction?
> ✔ What else do I need to know about each of these dimensions?

If, as a business owner, you can answer these four questions about every major area of your operation you're already well on your way. If, on the other hand, you need more information you are not alone. More than two-thirds of small businesses find gaps in their understanding on two or more dimensions of the pyramid. Now is the perfect time to fill in those gaps.

The Profit Pyramid™ Case Study

Edward was managing a light industrial firm that manufactured high-end tools for mining companies. His strategy, objectives, and goals were clear. So Edward wanted to know more about his measures. One of his favorite metrics was to decrease the cost-per-run on the production line; running a larger volume of units to spread the set-up time costs across more units effectively lowering the cost per unit. Mission accomplished, right? Not so fast. The large production runs created excess inventory, carrying costs, and increased floor space demands. The CFO stepped in to balance the current order size and forecasted orders with the fixed cost to set up the line and the associated costs to hold the excess inventory.

Now the performance measures are well balanced at the overall business level whereas before the previous measures were driving disjointed decisions in different and suboptimal directions. Customer value was considered in how long, on average, they would have to wait for a production run vs. purchasing directly from inventory. Performance measures across the pyramid now are front and foremost in the design of strategic and compatible measures at the company level. Profits flow to Edward's business from balancing cash, work-in-process, finished inventory, and production run size. When multiple measures compete or pull in different directions, use customer value and profits as the organizing framework for your analysis.

Strategic Alignment

Measures can track both external results and internal processes; the overarching goal is strategic alignment at the overall level of the business. It's common for measures to conflict when taken at the department, process, or micro level. Bottom-up optimization of individual detailed processes before the business goals are aligned at the entity level can lead to conflicting measures. The law of unintended consequences is at work here. The measures are best developed by the people closest to the process to help ensure full understanding of the situational context in which the performance measure will be applied. Test all measures for congruence with the other levels in the pyramid to make sure they support the business strategy. At the final stage, the most important items are alignment with customer value and profits.

Goals and Objectives

This is a good time to get clarity about your goals and objectives. Let's start with objectives. They bring your business strategy to life and focus on how to serve your customers in fulfilling the mission of your business. Customer satisfaction achieved through providing excellent customer service is a primary objective for all businesses, large and small.

> *... providing **excellent customer service** is a key objective for all businesses, large and small.*

Excellent customer service increases customer loyalty which can translate into goals for customer retention and referrals. Customer satisfaction keeps them coming back to you for more. Remember when you bought this book instead of going to a seminar, you saved on hotel and airfare; take the time and money you saved to get clear on your business goals and objectives.

Profitability is the second most common business objective. Achieving and maintaining profitability means ensuring that your revenues consistently exceed your total costs. Focus on controlling your costs across your entire value chain including: purchasing, capital equipment, maintenance, production, delivery, servicing, and collections while maintaining and expanding your profit margins. This objective is closely tied to productivity goals, both of your team and of your assets.

Growth is another important business objective. Treading water is a losing game. Profitable growth, not growth at all cost, is the byword. Effective execution is paramount. Growth requires the strategic application of your business assets toward viable profit opportunities. These assets include people, products, equipment, and funds as your goal could be to increase profitable growth by a target percentage while building a defensible and expanding competitive advantage.

Cash and working capital adequacy is essential for the survival of your business. Persistent cash squeezes spell trouble and limit your options to plan, provide excellent customer service, innovate, and grow. Effective management of cash and working capital and achievement of accounts payable goals is important.

Measures

When designing performance measures for your business, balance simplicity with effectiveness and data availability with relevance. One way to start reviewing your current performance measures is map them to your business strategy, goals and objectives in order to document:

✔ What is being measured now?
✔ How it is being measured?
✔ What are the sources of the data?
✔ How to interpret the data?
✔ What's working?
✔ What's not?
✔ What results are you looking for?

Based on what's working now, clarify what each measure makes visible – a window into the cost, value, and profit drivers of your business. Then step back and look at what you could be measuring. Begin to formulate new or modified performance measures based on new insights into the potential power of informed decision making and the subtle and not-so-subtle interactions of one business process with another. Keep working on potential performance measures until you cover one area in your business. Then pare down the measures to less than four. If you have too many measures, it all turns into meaningless stew.

Testing the Measures

After the measures have been redefined, vetted, and rationalized, it's time to test them. Reality sets in quickly if the measure that has been buffed and polished has moved too far off-the-mark from the process it was designed to measure. The person who owns the business process is best positioned to assess the effectiveness of the measure. If it's no longer valid, rework it. The second major consideration is ready data availability. To be effective the performance measures need to run like a machine – automatically presenting the data to you on a routine and consistent basis. Without a lot of extra effort. Without asking. Without fail.

Testing in the real world under normal operations of your business over a period of a few weeks can provide a clearer picture of the impact of the performance measure on your processes, products, customers, and profits. Make any required changes to your measures and test them again. Some measures can be stable for an extended time while others need to reflect market dynamics and must be reviewed for relevance and accuracy more frequently.

Results

Now that your performance measures have been designed and tested, they must be implemented, and more importantly, applied. There's a joke in the self-help genre that designates all of the thousands of unused programs and seminar workbooks as "shelf-help". Don't let your performance measures fall into that abyss. Above all, you're looking for results. Verifiable results. Indisputable results.

Establish a schedule noting what information is to be run, when, and who is to be on the distribution list. Then follow up routinely and aggressively. Manage by exception. Fix the outliers and get to the bottom of each situation. Maybe a one-off aberration comes to your attention or maybe there's a deep underlying problem to be uncovered and addressed. Either way, the sooner you know the better.

The new performance measures will show you results that you've never seen before. There could be a critical flaw in your business model. Perhaps your costing and discounting strategies are hurting profits. The numbers can provide early warnings to unexpected decreases in sales as orders begin to lag behind projections, unrelated to seasonal variations. Excess rework is a negative result, for example, that can indicate that the order intake process with specifications needs to be more detailed.

Performance Measures → Results → Customer Value → Profits

Customer Value

Look at each of your candidate performance measures with the overarching objective to increase customer value. Make the needed changes. Systematize it. Continue to refine the system as needed as you go along. Keep it going. It's a new way to manage your business – forever. To analyze business decisions. To measure profitability. To allocate resources efficiently. To increase customer value. To boost profits.

CHAPTER 6

KEY AREAS TO CHECK FOR PROFIT LEAKS

The big things ARE the little things.
Teresa Amabile and Steven Kramer

In any business, there are almost always hidden and potential profit sources resulting from profit leaks. Generally they are hiding in plain sight. Some vary from business to business. Others are universal. How do you find these profit leaks and minimize them for your company? Here are six common places to look for profit leaks in your business.

Profit Leak #1: Purchasing

You could be paying too much for what you buy or buying things you don't need. When you analyze your buying patterns from suppliers, explore the option of earning bundle pricing and cumulative quantity discounts. Look over your purchases from your major suppliers over the period of one year. In many cases, concentrating your purchases with a single vendor can pay big dividends. You'll be playing on a larger field by buying what you were going to buy anyway. Negotiate increasing discounts for increasing volumes and earn them as you go. It's a win-win for both you and your supplier. It definitely shows up in your profit and loss statement. In other cases where special discounts are not available to you, it might be more advantageous to shop around for the best price on each item separately. You can go back to the original supplier and offer to buy more for a better price if they're willing to negotiate. Supplier relationships can play a very important role in the consistent delivery of value to your customers. Reliable suppliers can be true partners in your business. In many cases, total purchasing can be cut with no impact on the business. Effective purchasing can boost your bottom line.

Profit Leak #2: Credit

One of the most important ways to maximize profit in your business is to explore ways to reduce the interest expense on outstanding funds from high-cost sources. Analyze all of your credit sources noting rates and amounts. Rearrange or reschedule terms where possible. Pay down any loan carrying an excessive interest rate working from highest to lowest. Work with your customers to accelerate in-bound payments and collections. Consider offering discounts to your customers for early payments where practical and consider requiring deposits before you begin work, if feasible. Work with your suppliers to delay out-bound payments where desirable. The savings you reap from effective credit and cash management will flow directly to your bottom line and greatly reduce the fear of running out of cash that we've all felt before. Secure lower-cost financing as soon as you can to replace expensive sources.

Profit Leak #3: Transaction Costs

Analyze the buying patterns of your top 20 customers over the past year and you can definitely discover potential hidden profit opportunities. What are your customers buying and why? When are they buying? Drill down into that data and apply problem solving skills. Is there potential to increase order size or to bundle orders with other products? There could be significant transaction processing cost savings there. If your product is an essential component of theirs, your customer's forecast can be closely aligned with your forecast to increase order predictability. Explore ways to customize quantities to decrease your order processing and shipping costs. And look for opportunities for your customers to offer your product to their customers. Match your data with your insights to gain a unique perspective on your business - a true competitive advantage. You can boost your profits when you begin to track underlying trends in your transaction data.

Profit Leak #4 – Training and Travel Costs

When sales and orders are coming in a little slower, you might be tempted to try some untested training techniques. In many businesses, effective skills acquisition is instrumental to producing sales and thus generating a profit. But too often many business owners get caught up in networking events, seminars, and other meetings that don't directly boost skills or drive sales to the bottom line. One way to control these costs is to plan training needs six to twelve months in advance. That way you won't be susceptible to the next out-of-town seminar advertisement that promises you the equivalent of making $1 million while you sleep. It's a great idea to selectively enrich and expand your skills. The marketplace is changing rapidly and you need to be at the top of your game. But the decision to attend a training event should be driven by your needs (on a demand basis), rather than reacting to an offer out of the blue (on a supply basis). Acquire skills for you and your team immediately before you need them.

Profit Leak #5: – Facility Costs

Some businesses expand their space too quickly using optimistic growth projections; other businesses face an unexpected decline in volume. In either case these businesses find themselves with excess facility costs. Oftentimes these excess costs cannot be passed on to the customer due to competition in the marketplace. If you're considering expanding, plan your volume out over the next two years and perform a sensitivity analysis on your estimates. In other words, what would happen if your numbers are off by 10 or 20% up or down? Will the expansion still be cost-effective or does this shift make expansion unwarranted at this time? If you're now faced with excess space consider creative ways to expand your volume. Perhaps introducing a product extension would be advisable. Perhaps you could process orders for other firms to help defray the cost of the space. Or consider renting out some of your space for storage in the short term. Check for any flexibility in your lease with your landlord. Plan out long term to either retain or shed the excess space based on projected volumes, estimated costs, and predicted profits. The key is to plug the short-term profit leak.

Profit Leak #6 – Telecomm Costs

Just as in facilities, some businesses expand their telecommunications costs too quickly to be absorbed by the current and near-term sales volume. Business owners are almost universally optimistic or else they wouldn't go into business in the first place. Yet unbridled optimism can lead these businesses into that trap of excess telecommunication costs. Committed in a contract with too many functions, too many features, too many options, and too many units is an expensive place to be. You may be forced to ride out your contracts until expiration or there might be a way to negotiate the fees for a better rate. Next time, buy only what you need and talk about adding on. Most vendors will gladly increase your order, but few will decrease it.

Potential Leaks within Your Business

Now it's time to explore potential profit leaks within your operations. Watch out for these six internal profit leaks as you review your business. These common profit leaks, and many others, can begin to stimulate your thinking. Remember, cost savings go straight to the bottom line of your income statement. Presented below are six more common sources of profit leaks in your business; there are literally dozens of others. Consider the impact of each of these potential internal profit leaks in your business.

6 Common Internal Profit Leak Areas

✔ Product Features
✔ Customer Requests
✔ Unexpected Add-ons
✔ Aggressive Pricing
✔ Incomplete Costing
✔ Unreliable Systems

In each of these internal profit leak areas, there could be excessive costs building in your business. They often sneak in under the cover of darkness. Look back and notice any gradual changes over the past year where you were asked to add unexpected product features. Be on the lookout for special customer requests and add-ons; they often cost you far more than you realize. Note the occasions where you dropped your price to win an award; track the longer-term impacts of that decision. Step back and look to cover all of your costs, not just variable costs, in taking on new orders. And identify circumstances where you acted on data generated by your systems and it turned out to be wrong. This will get you started to think about your own potential profit leaks.

Customer Profitability

Another area of your business to review is your customers. What does it cost you to acquire a new customer? Are they somewhat homogeneous or are they vastly different? Do they use your products in similar ways? If your offering requires on-site visits, are they located close by or far away? Identify customers who are a drain on your resources and raise prices on those so demanding that they cause you to lose money, then keep on going down the list. Charge more or do less, those are the two profit boosting options. What is the best performance that you can expect from each of these areas? What questions could you be asking to get the information that you need?

Take this information and use it systematically in priority order for your business. Often where there is a burning issue, management focuses 100% of attention in that one area. That's fine during the period of crisis, but as soon as practicable thereafter start a round robin of high-level issues needed to keep your business running smoothly so that one area is not neglected for inordinate periods of time. This provides a window into the overall operation of your business. Management by exception is completely scalable. It can be used at the strategic level of the overall business and it can also be used to analyze individual products, business processes, and customers.

Your Current Business Profile

Now that you've been thinking about your business in new ways, it's very helpful to establish your baseline. In order to accurately track how much progress you will make with these profit boosting techniques, it's essential to know where you are now. The first step on the road to reach your Peak Profit Potential is to complete a brief profile for your business as it is now, a snapshot of the current situation. A convenient template is provided below. The **Background Information** section collects information about your business, your products, and your customers. The **Financial Information** section collects the last three years of annual revenues and gross profits. The **Strategy Information** section poses questions regarding your number one profit challenge, how long you've had it, and what mechanisms you have tried to overcome it. This provides a valuable baseline for your business as it stands today. Collect this vital information about your business.

Your Current Business Profile

BACKGROUND INFORMATION

Business Name	
Date Formed	
Business Description	
Industry	
Major Financing & Rate	
Number of Employees	
Total # of Products	
Top 3 Products by Volume	
Top 3 Products by Profits	
Total # of Customers	
Top 3 Customers by Volume	
Top 3 Customers by Profits	

FINANCIAL INFORMATION

| Annual Revenues Over the Past 3 Years | |
| Annual Gross Profits Over the Past 3 Years | |

KEY AREAS TO CHECK FOR PROFIT LEAKS

	Strategy Information
Where do your customers think you provide value?	
What is your #1 profit challenge?	
Is this a temporary profit challenge?	
How long has it been a profit challenge?	
How does this profit challenge affect your business?	
What have you tried in the past to overcome this?	
What has worked?	
What hasn't worked?	
What could you do if this profit challenge was resolved?	
On a scale of 1-10, how committed are you to boost your profits now?	

CHAPTER 7

PEAK: THE FOUR-STEP PROGRAM TO PLUG PROFIT LEAKS

There is at least one point in the history of any company when you have to change dramatically to rise to the next level of performance. Miss that moment and you start to decline.
Andy Grove

Over the past three decades as I was working for scores of high-end consulting clients, I was researching, gathering, and analyzing the information that I'm sharing with you now. From this extensive research and experience, I developed a four-step program to plug profit leaks. In order to reach your Peak Profit Potential, these leaks must be plugged. Before only the big boys had access to business performance measurement tools; now you can use the same methods to help boost profits in your business. By using these same strategies you can achieve the same results in your business – a profitability boost. The four-step program presented here is a systematic, proven, and practical approach to identify, analyze, and remedy profit leaks in your business.

The next four chapters detail each of the profit boost steps in turn to first plug the holes where money is leaking out of your business and then to progressively move on to more specific profit maximization opportunities. These opportunities are different for each business but they have the same themes: knowing what's working, knowing what's not, then doing the right things right.

Here is an overview of the four-step program that forms the acronym PEAK:

Step 1 P = Prepare an Inventory

Prepare an inventory of areas where your business could be leaking money. This action documents where you are today. This first action is critical in order to set the baseline and begin to measure the impact of the decisions that you are currently making in your business. In most businesses some things are working very well, some things marginally well, and some things not so much. After the leaks are documented, it is time to move to the second step.

Step 2 E = Estimate the Leaks

Estimate how much money is leaking from each source. In this step you begin to quantify the profit leaks in your business. Money is likely to be leaking from multiple sources in varied quantities for various reasons at various times. The first priority is to discover the biggest leak where your profit margins are eroding. This is a powerful step to estimate the size of the most problematic leaks in your business that are draining your profits. This action guides your primary attention and resources where they are needed most.

Step 3 A = Articulate the Options

Articulate options to plug the biggest leak. This action directs your thinking from the past toward the future. Now that the primary leaks in your business have been identified and quantified, focus on the biggest one. It's time to plug it. Identify options and areas where you can tighten up business processes and systems around the leak. You might be quite surprised how your business processes have degraded over time. Envision and explore your options to streamline and rejuvenate them. Be open in coming up with techniques to fill the gaps. This is a brainstorming exercise. Get creative and have fun.

Step 4 K = Kickstart Your Action Plan

Kickstart an action plan to plug the biggest leak. This step takes some of the most promising ideas from the envisioning activity cited in step three and prioritizes them for action in the upcoming year. Many business processes can be streamlined or modified while some processes that are no longer serving their purpose can be eliminated altogether. The action plan focuses specifically on activities that will get your business back on track for Peak Profit Potential, and fast. When combined, these actions will set your business on a new profit course. Systematize the actions and track your progress, one leak at a time. This step applies the new profit strategy to your business in real-time, and finely tunes it to achieve a systematic, consistent, and reliable processes for you to manage your business in new ways with new visibility to boost profits. Then, when you're ready, you have the tools to do it all over again to boost your profits even more.

CHAPTER 8

P: PREPARE AN INVENTORY WHERE YOUR BUSINESS COULD BE LEAKING MONEY

All truths are easy to understand once they are discovered;
the point is to discover them. Galileo Galilei

Throughout the early chapters of the book, we busted some myths, provided company case studies, and listed multiple examples of common profit leaks in other businesses. Now it's time to apply the 4-step PEAK program analysis to your business.

Let's explore the first step, **Prepare an inventory of areas where your business could be leaking money.** By taking inventory of what is happening in your business today you'll gain valuable insights. It will begin to illuminate what is actually happening in your business vs. what you may think is happening. This is a detective exercise designed to explore your processes, products, services, customers, vendors, credit, sales, costs, and profits in a new light. You now have the opportunity to stand back and view your business operations from above to gain a new perspective of where the choke points might be. Where rework is needed and why. Where communications are not effective and where the ball gets dropped. You can explore these areas yourself, then you can ask your customers, suppliers, and other members of your team. All of these inputs will be helpful for you to sort through, validate or repudiate, and then prioritize.

Possible Profit Leaks

Every business is different and so the sources of profit leaks can vary widely. There are patterns within overall industries that might provide some specific clarifying insights while some other concepts are more universal across business types. Chapter Six covered many types of common profit leaks. In filling out your Current Business Profile you stated your biggest profitability challenge. This is a good starting point for your analysis. Begin with the primary activity in your business. What is it that you regularly produce for your customers? "Produce" is a general term encompassing a wide range of business areas including: service delivery, training, information products, coaching, consulting, construction, manufacturing, and many other types of businesses. Look at your major sources of revenue and see where the money comes in. Observe what it takes to get the final "products" out the door and delivered to the customer. To what extent are things running smoothly, predictably, and profitably?

In working with Fortune 500 clients, one area that plagues both manufacturers and service providers is excess work-in-process; this is a major source for potential profit leaks. Work that is not yet completed has already accumulated costs, often substantial costs. Identifying the reasons that work is lingering too long as work-in-process before moving to finished goods is an area ripe for analysis in businesses of all types and sizes. Many projects languish in the 85-95% complete range where they fall short of completion and payment, and thus profits. What takes longer than it should in your business?

There are also important clues in your last cash flow statement, income statement, and balance sheet. One of these statements without the others conceals the full picture. For example, partially writing down accounts receivable will hurt the balance sheet yet might improve short-term cash flow. Building up accounts receivable looks good on the balance sheet - more assets, yet it is not so good for the business. Every part of your business is linked to many other parts of your business. They are inextricably linked – so the entire picture is needed to make informed decisions.

The chart shows some common areas for profit leaks in small businesses.

Common Profit Leaks

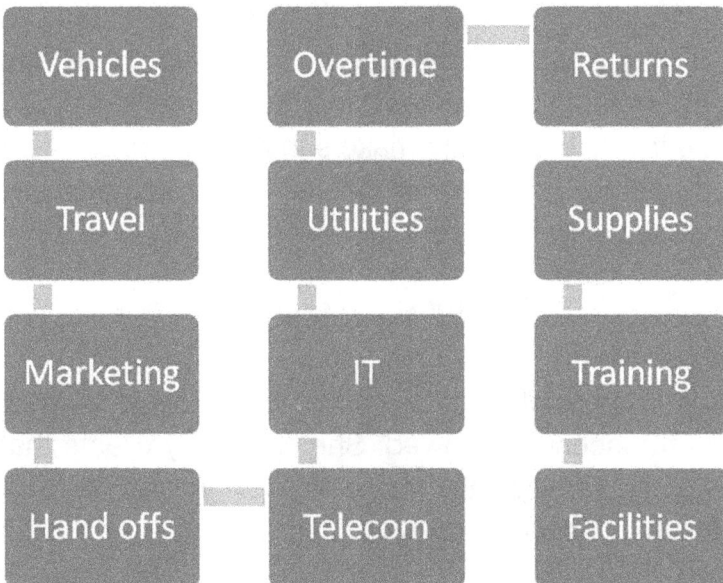

Vehicles	Overtime	Returns
Travel	Utilities	Supplies
Marketing	IT	Training
Hand offs	Telecom	Facilities

In this step, the goal is for you to make a list of potential profit leaks in order to identify the major profit leaks in your business in order of importance. You can come back and revisit this "P" step over and over as you move down the list to plug more and more of the major profit leaks. And the good news is that all the money saved goes straight to your bottom line.

Items that go on your list can include the ones in the chart and you can add your own to tailor your inventory list to your business. List all the possible leaks that you can think of. This is really a brainstorming exercise; you'll get the chance to prioritize it later. One important dimension of your business is cash adequacy. Even profitable businesses can get into a cash squeeze when suppliers demand quick payment and your customers are slow to pay. It's critical to resolve cash issues first because they're the number one killer of small businesses. Yes profits are important, but as they say, cash is king.

Capital adequacy is another important dimension that can be revealed by doing cash flow forecasting to make sure that your business has a sufficient buffer to meet your cash demands month after month without fear, without worry. It's difficult to be profitable if you're forced to make substandard decisions due to a lack of capital. Your level of capital and ready cash can help you to strategically manage your cost of credit.

"P" Case Study

Connie is a financial planner who began to face revenue pressures as the economy slowed. She has many clients that seek out her team's services and they often want to meet face-to-face. The retirees on her client list really appreciate the personal touch.

Connie signed a three-year lease for office space where she and six other planners could meet clients, hold meetings, and catch up on new products and trends. But the fixed costs of the space were taking an increasing toll on her profit margins. When going through this exercise to build an inventory, Connie listed six major sources of potential profit leaks.

- ✔ Space
- ✔ Utilities
- ✔ Processes
- ✔ Supplies
- ✔ Credit
- ✔ Marketing

The space and utilities are closely related expenses that appear to be outpacing their share of total expenses given Connie's current and projected revenues. Processes cover a wide area and need to be further broken down into Client Management which includes: client intake, initial planning, revised planning, monitoring, and communications. Usage of supplies is unconstrained and the quantity of materials, brochures, paper, toner, and other supplies is on the rise. She wants to take a look at her cost of credit now even though it was never an issue before. And, in Connie's view, marketing costs are too high; they made her list of top potential profit leaks.

The Inventory as Starting Point

The inventory is the most important step in the PEAK 4-step program. It provides an opportunity for introspection and for collecting information about different aspects of your business, some of which you might not have reviewed for several years. In many businesses, processes initiated for a specific product or a customer request may no longer serve your needs. Not only might they be inefficient but they could also be costing you money. Wouldn't it be nice to know if an inefficient process is leaking profits when your customers don't perceive or appreciate the added value?

Categories of Business Expenses

Take a quick look at your income statement and you'll see the major categories of business expenses. Next, drill down a level on a line item that you're interested in or on an area that might have caught you by surprise. Scan all of your expenses. See their relative sizes when compared to all of your other expenses. Select areas of interest to explore in your inventory analysis.

Let's look at one line item, for example, supplies. If this is a larger number than you expected, drill down to expose any abuse or waste. Other common expense items can be rich areas to mine as well. Each business is different and some expenses vary seasonally. Sometimes you're locked into contracts and no quick changes can be made. This isn't about just quick fixes, although they can sometimes make a big impact if signs of waste or inefficiency jump right off the page. The goal is to become more aware of the important drivers of your business. What's flowing in, what's flowing out, when, and why. Keeping an eye out for profit leaks involves tracking them to the source.

Assess Process Complexity

What you're doing might no longer be working as well as it was before, or it might not be working at all. How you're doing things might not be as effective as it could be, or there might be a better way altogether. If you don't have performance measures in place, you won't be able to tell for sure whether small shifts in what you're doing and how you're doing it are producing the results you expect. That's why we identify potential profit leaks.

Another multi-faceted area in which to identify profit leaks is your business processes. Any activity that doesn't directly result in increased customer value is a candidate for careful review. Look for complexity in your products or services along your full value chain. Connie will be looking at five service life cycle process steps in her Client Management from client-intake all the way through to client monitoring and communications. Do your current business processes fully align both with customer needs and your profitability targets? Do they fit together to meet customer needs over your product or service life cycle?

Get Started

The tools embodied in the 4-step PEAK program provide an easy-to-use guide for you to get started. The inventory worksheet can be located at *www.PeakProfitPotential.com/inventory*. If you have any questions while you're doing the analysis leave a comment at www.*PeakProfitPotential.com* and I will collect your questions and post them in an FAQ section on my website.

One way business owners can quickly prepare their inventory is to set aside some time over the next couple weeks to get this done. You know your schedule better than anyone else so whether blocking off half-days or two-hour appointments would work better for you. Bite off manageable segments and keep at it until the job is done. Get the help you need from the people you need such as your accountant, banker, customers, or staff.

If your business is in a severe cash or profit squeeze I recommend that you set aside the time you need right away. The sooner you begin, the sooner you will reap the rewards of increased profitability. If your business is both profitable and stable, schedule your inventory as a high priority task balanced with other essential activities that require your attention. You know when you work best. Are you the type to get this done quickly by completely rearranging your schedule, committing a couple of hours on a Saturday, or would it be better to block out fixed appointment times over the next two weeks?

After you complete your inventory take a look at it and note any areas that surprise you. See where you were well-informed and where you weren't. It's quite an interesting exercise. And it sets the foundation for the Peak Profit Potential program – a powerful business improvement system. You will never look at your business the same way again.

You'll get great benefits from just this first step alone, especially if you've haven't looked at your business processes in quite a while. It's worth staying focused. The light at the end of the tunnel is increased profits. The way to do that is to get your arms around your data. What could possibly be a better use of your time than identifying potential profit leaks in your business?

CHAPTER 9

E: ESTIMATE HOW MUCH IS LEAKING FROM EACH SOURCE

What counts can't always be counted; what can be counted doesn't always count. Albert Einstein

Now that you've completed your inventory of potential profit leaks, it's time to go into more detail on each of the items. It's time to estimate how much money is leaking from each item on your list. This can be done in several ways. On the first pass, many business owners simply come up with a number in their heads that seems reasonable. They have a sense of how much excess cost can be wrung out of the process. Some areas don't lend themselves to easy estimation and more data is needed to quantify the answer. In other cases, you can come up with a guess but don't have a great degree of confidence in it, and more data is needed.

"E" Case Study

Connie, the financial planner, analyzed each item on her list and provided estimates of excess costs. One of the areas in her business where she was very unsure of her costs was in her Customer Management processes, so she drilled down to five steps that comprise the client experience.

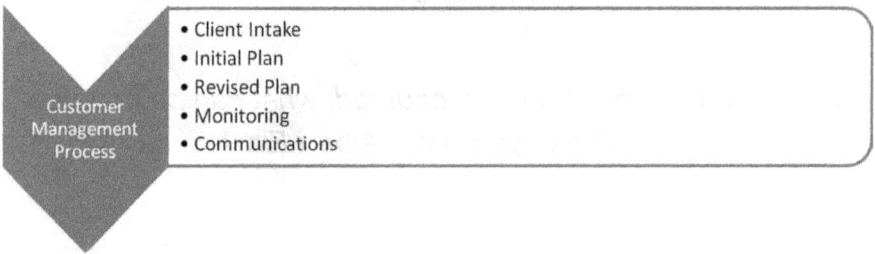

Customer Management Process

- Client Intake
- Initial Plan
- Revised Plan
- Monitoring
- Communications

For the client intake process, Connie used standard forms to collect the detailed financial information that she needed. Some clients filled them out completely and correctly on the first pass, but most didn't. They often brought in incomplete forms, incorrect forms, or no forms at all. In these cases, the first meeting was not so much about getting the whole picture of where the client was and where they wanted to go. Instead, much time was spent on tracking down missing information such as the value of IRAs and company retirement accounts. So Connie began her costing estimations in the Customer Management Process.

Customer Management Process

Here's how Connie got the answers she needed for her business. She first estimated the total number of new clients per year. She has been pursuing an aggressive speaking and advertising campaign and it is really bringing in the clients. Given her recent track record, Connie assumed six new clients per month, for each of six planners, in 12 months. That is : 6 x 6 x 12 = 432 intakes per year. Then she began to break it down by the percentages of clients and the varying levels of completeness in their forms. Fully 70% of new clients had issues with the intake forms, which is 302 clients. She then broke them down into various percentages of clients using three different levels of incomplete forms.

% of incomplete and missing forms = 70% x 432 = 302 incompletes per year

10% very incomplete forms =	10% x 302 = 31 very incomplete
60% somewhat incomplete forms =	60% x 302 = 181 some-what incomplete
30% almost complete forms =	30% x 302 = 90 almost complete forms

Time value of a planner hour = $100

Time required for incomplete = 1 hr	1 hr x 31 x $100 = $3,100
Time required for somewhat incomplete = ½ hr	½ hr x 181 x $100 = $9,550
Time required for almost complete = ¼ hr	¼ hr x 90 x $100 = $2,250

Connie viewed the calculations with surprise and interest. She thought that more money was lost on the clients with very incomplete forms. And in one way it is; it costs $100 in extra time per client. But only 10% of the clients bring in very incomplete forms. What Connie discovered is that there is huge savings potential if she could markedly reduce the number of somewhat incomplete forms. Fully 60% of new clients with incomplete forms are classified as "somewhat incomplete" and these require ½ hour of unexpected planner time that is not fully factored into her costs. In this economic and competitive environment, there was little room for her to raise her prices. She had to cut her costs. So Connie dug deeper and pulled out trends noting common issues and gaps that this group of clients was having with their intake forms.

Your Estimate of Profit Leaks

How about your business? Take each line of your profit leak inventory one at a time. Begin to work the list to identify the biggest potential sources of profits and develop informed estimates for each line. For example, if shipping is one of your excess costs for some of your products, is it possible to reduce costs by 10, 20 or even 30%? Be aggressive yet realistic in your estimates on each line item. Realize that many costs cannot be eliminated, only managed.

In many cases, there are a few obvious quick fixes that can be implemented immediately for instant payback. Don't you just love it when that happens? In the rest of the cases, others may take a little more digging.

Quantify your potential profit leaks. Assess when that leak occurs. Connie, our financial planner, found that her intake process was fraught with expensive time killers. But intake is only one stage of her Client Management process; she found most of her other processes were on track. You might find wide variances between tight, consistent, and efficient processes and loose, variable, and inefficient ones.

Get a clearer picture of your business processes and the inner workings of your business. Are your leaks related to a specific product, process, or purchase? Are your leaks associated with a specific customer? Is the leak continuous or intermittent? It's important to carefully document the conditions under which the leak is occurring. Follow Connie's example to drill down to make sure that as you prepare your estimates you understand what's going on, when it's happening, and what percentage of your transactions are involved.

At first estimating your profit leaks and sources might appear to be a daunting task; I encourage you to keep with it. It can be incredibly rewarding. It can change your entire business, especially if you're operating on a razor-thin profit margin. Use the information that's already compiled. One of the most important sources of information is your recent financial statements; your latest tax return might also be helpful. Connie's example shows how simple it can be to identify and estimate potential profit leaks. She will cycle back and do the profit leak inventory again and again as she completes the PEAK process. You can too.

Be Selective

Avoid the natural temptation to dive in at first glance, stop the exercise in midstream, and chop your marketing and advertising budget right off the bat. Perhaps these are dollars well spent; perhaps they're not. Effective marketing is an expense and it's also an investment in the future. Only a results-based analysis of your Return on Investment (ROI) will tell you whether your marketing money is well spent. Put these costs on the list if they're a concern to you and analyze them with all the rest.

Intermittent Leak Case Study

Matthew's medical technician firm found that a major profit leak was intermittent and thus difficult to pin down. The leak only happened when a big customer expected rush service. The team of technicians did everything they could to get the job done including pressuring suppliers for expedited order processing for testing equipment, overnight package deliveries, working extra hours, and other time-saving methods to meet the deadline. Even though the customer really appreciated this fantastic service, this special treatment exploded Matthew's costs without a concomitant rise in the price. A major profit leak indeed. With all good intentions, Matthew's team was trying to serve and satisfy an important customer - but at a loss. Many more of these transactions and Matthew will be out of business.

From this exercise Matthew discovered that:

- ✔ What do you don't know can hurt you
- ✔ What your team doesn't know can hurt you
- ✔ What your team doesn't tell you can hurt you.

Fixed Price Leak Case Study

Andrew ran a business strategy consulting practice for mid-tier firms. He became quite skilled at marketing a fixed price service called *Business Strategy Reboot*. He allocated hours to documenting the client's industry and competitive environment, analyzing the client's offerings and business practices, and drafting new strategy options to increase market share. His deliverable was a series of spreadsheets along with a presentation and briefing of three viable options and their respective impacts on market share. By working closely with the client, Andrew's team produced dozens of successful engagements each year.

But last year, the profit picture changed. Andrew's team got caught in the telecom industry where the regulations and practices were changing rapidly. Whereas a normal assignment would wrap up in approximately four or five months, two assignments were dragging on much longer because strategy options that were agreed upon just two weeks earlier were no longer possible. This required extensive rework by Andrew's team. Andrew's fixed price contracts did not take this possibility into account and was forced to redo the assignments. This was a major profit squeeze because the teams could not move on to their new assignments that were already in the pipeline. This lost time could never be recouped. Andrew then quantified the profit leak:

24 hours rework x $200 per hour x 2 weeks = **$9,600** for one job

Cost of the incident	Frequency		Estimated Profit Leak
$9,600	x 2	=	$19,200

The Underlying Nature of Leaks

After you begin to more fully understand the nature of the potential profit leak in your business and when and how it occurs, you're in a better position to estimate how much money is actually leaking. Run your numbers. Estimate the potential profit leaks and identify your number one source. If the profit leak is related to a particular product, service, or customer, find the data you need based on other profitable transactions or simply do a mini-P&L for the transaction in question. Oftentimes prices cannot be raised. In these cases, it's imperative to control your costs and keep them aligned with your targets. In other cases such as Matthew's the offering can be repackaged, as in adding a rush service premium to restore the activity to profitability. In Andrew's case, he changed the terms of his contracts to include provisions to address seismic shifts in the industry. Unless the offering is a strategic loss leader, something needs to be done and fast to minimize and plug the profit leak.

Focus on one transaction at a time. What should the cost be to produce and deliver the offering vs. the actual cost? What is the source of your information? How reliable is the information or is it just a guess? If your information is not reliable, peel back the process elements to reveal more details. When the offering was first envisioned, what were the estimated labor, material, and resource inputs? What is the estimated leak amount? How many of these type of transactions per month? For example, if you've estimated $10 in profit leaks for a single product in transit and you produce one of them per day, which is 20 per month, then:

Amount of leak = $10 x 20 transactions per month = $200 monthly profit leak

Modify this process and this formula to accommodate your specific needs. As you gather more data, the total picture of the leaks and their relationships to business processes as well as to other leaks will become clearer. Are the major leaks one time vs. persistent? How many times do they occur per month?

At the end of this step, you will see your inventory of profit leaks along with the estimated dollar values associated with them. Select your top leak or group of leaks to carry forward to the next step in the PEAK strategy.

CHAPTER 10

A: ARTICULATE OPTIONS TO PLUG THE TOP LEAK

Be bold. If you're going to make an error, make a doozey, and don't be afraid to hit the ball. Billie Jean King

Oftentimes from the estimation step you have a good idea as to how to plug the top leak. If you can see the best way already, then go ahead and plug the leak. If you are not sure, here are a few options you can consider.

Options

✔ Start doing something new
✔ Stop doing something
✔ Do something differently
✔ Combine several steps
✔ Have someone else do it
✔ Combinations and other options.

The next six sections of this chapter explore each of these options in turn with specific company examples.

Start Doing Something New Case Study

In Andrew's case, the method to plug the profit leak was clear. He reworked his *Business Strategy Reboot* contract to state that after the client signed off on the proposed strategies, any rework after that would proceed on a time-and-materials basis. Andrew needed to remove the risk of unlimited change orders from his business practices even as he retained his core practice of delivering on fixed price contracts. Andrew successfully plugged the profit leak.

Stop Doing Something Case Study

David ran a firm that provided home health services to amateur athletes undergoing extensive rehabilitation. In some cases, the patient was not quite ready for their appointment. To run the business at a profit the schedule was designed to be tight and efficient. There were six patients a day to see plus driving time, which was quite unpredictable. The scheduling team did their best to book the appointments to allow adequate drive time to get to the next patient with the rehab specialist arriving on time and unharried. When the patients were not quite ready, the rehab specialist would wait and then extend the appointment time. This put a squeeze on the time allotment for the next patient and left the rehab specialists quite harried. At the end of the day, they had worked too many hours and were due overtime. This had to stop.

David initiated a call-up service where the rehab specialist would confirm the appointment when they were on their way from their previous appointment. They would arrive on time and leave on time and the patient would be responsible for any gaps in insurance coverage. This step dramatically reduced the number of late appointments. And it stopped a major profit leak for David's company. What can you stop doing?

Do Something Differently Case Study

Roger ran an engineering design firm. His work required many updates during the design process. The team met with the client on site and reviewed the issues, challenges, and requirements. Normally, the team would meet with the client face-to-face about five or six times throughout the design process. It turned out to be very time consuming, especially for quick updates where there were no pressing issues to discuss.

Roger replaced three face-to-face meetings with videoconferences using remote file sharing technologies. They could communicate or meet with the client more often which greatly improved technical results for the client and produced significant cost savings for Roger's company. A true win-win. What can you do differently even if it's only some of the time?

Combine Several Steps Case Study

Melanie, a successful high-end regional produce broker would meet with the clients first to note specific requirements and document the critical differentiators for what would satisfy their produce needs. She would rank their purchasing criteria

*… communicate with the client more often which greatly **improved results**…*

based on quality, appearance, size, taste, quantity, delivery, and other dimensions based on the specific produce item. After this process was complete to the client's satisfaction, Melanie would go back to her office and identify suppliers based on availability and proceed to match up the orders. She'd go back the client with sources and quantities and dimensions and tradeoffs. This process took several days and was working well yet was quite inefficient.

To streamline this work while still maintaining the highest quality, Melanie prepared a pre-order sheet for the client to complete in advance of their meeting noting which items they were seeking, what quality they were looking for, and in what quantities. She posted this product information on her website and automatically notified her primary suppliers. The suppliers responded to the pre-order information with real time quotes of product quality, availability, and pricing. Under this new process, when Melanie met with the client they actually firmed up the orders saving days for both the client and Melanie. A significant cost savings and a profit boost for Melanie's company until her competitors catch up. What steps can you combine in your business?

Have Someone Else Do It

There are many examples of having someone else do the work that needs to be done. At McDonalds, we clean our own tables. At Southwest Airlines, we book our own tickets on line. At United Airlines at Dulles Airport, we carry our own checked baggage from the ticket counter over to the baggage loading area after the agent weighs it and before TSA screens it. At medical offices, we fill out four different forms asking for our names and health information to make it easier for them to file it. At many rental car companies, we fill in an on-line form in advance to check in and select any extra coverages. Then at the rental counter it takes less than a minute to pick up the car and be on your way; some companies avoid the counter altogether. Work can be transferred to suppliers, customers, or other third parties. What activities in your business can logically be transferred to others without sacrificing quality and service?

Combinations and Other Options

There are a myriad of ways that businesses can streamline their operations. The five examples presented above merely scratch the surface. Each business is different, yet the fundamental principles of efficiency and effectiveness are the same. Rebecca runs a professional organizing service for law firms who were mishandling paper. She used three of the options to: start doing something new, stop doing something, and doing something differently. Rebecca pre-screened her clients better to reduce the tire kickers for her offer of a free 3-hour consult. She introduced a new on-line form that they filled out before her first contact with them. She stopped explaining her services to unqualified prospects and instead sent them to her website supported by a detailed introductory video and an extensive FAQ section.

> *... She stopped explaining her services to* **unqualified prospects** *...*

Get Creative with Your Options

Get creative when exploring options to plug the top leak in your business. What simple things can you do to make your business more efficient and more effective? If viable strategies did not reveal themselves, you can ask others in your industry at networking meetings, post a question on Linked-In, look for forms and templates on the web, send out a survey, or sit down with your team, possibly including customers or suppliers, to sort through the business process in question. Whatever method you choose, it's well worth it to get to the bottom of it and plug a profit leak using any combination of these approaches.

CHAPTER 11

K: KICKSTART AN ACTION PLAN TO PLUG THE TOP LEAK

Massive action is a cure all. Tony Robbins

Now that you know what leak you're plugging first and how you're going to plug it, it's time to kickstart an action plan including an activity list and associated due dates. The number one success factor in an action plan is that has to fit into the life you're already leading. You're already busy now.

If you're in crisis mode, and your plan has you doing something new for 20 hours a week, step back and make sure if that's what needs to be done that it indeed can be done. And it's essential to specify what else has to give. Unless you're at work reading mystery novels 20 hours a week, something's got to go, at least temporarily while you execute your action plan.

In ongoing businesses, most action plans are incremental and target the business owner's time no more than eight hours a week. Of course, this is highly variable. The point I'm making is that if you make a plan, be sure that it's realistic so that you actually can do it. Unfulfilled plans are a drain on precious resources and lead to even more discouragement. You can delegate action plan tasks to your team, just use caution. Don't overcommit yourself or anyone else or your action plan will fade into the oblivion of all of the other workplace clutter that constantly plagues us.

To get started on your action plan you can use a pen and paper, planning software, calendaring, worksheets, your phone, whiteboards, or any other tools that work for you. The main actions are to:

✔ Lay out the tasks
✔ Be specific
✔ Set objective criteria
✔ Assign dates
✔ Assign resources

As your action plan begins to come together, assess the entire plan. Validate that each step is doable and realistic. Specify how you'll monitor your action plan. Articulate how you'll adjust your action plan. Identify how much slack is included in the schedule and what you'd do if slippages occurred.

After your action plan is validated, it's time to get started on implementation. It's important that you commit the required time and resources to your plan not only from the outset, but also as it becomes a part of your regular management routine. After your action plan is underway, systematize the actions and track your progress. Note any initial bumps in the road and make the necessary adjustments. When you start a new way of doing things, it's important to build a system around it. Just like a new habit. The action plan should happen automatically. Plugging profit leaks is not a one-time endeavor. It will also work for you many times in the future. After you eliminate your top profit leak you will no longer be draining resources at the same rate as before. You can move on to plug the next profit leak on your inventory all the while boosting your profits. Take a look again at your Business Profile to track the impacts of this first PEAK analysis. What has shifted? What do you know now that you might not have known before?

	Post PEAK Round 1 Strategy Information
Where do your customers think you provide value?	
What is your #1 profit challenge?	
Is this a temporary profit challenge?	
How long has it been a profit challenge?	
How does this profit challenge affect your business?	
What have you tried in the past to overcome this?	
What has worked?	
What hasn't worked?	
What could you do if this profit challenge was resolved?	
On a scale of 1-10, how committed are you to boost your profits now?	

The PEAK Cycle Repeats

After you've completed one cycle of the PEAK program, you'll have everything you need to do it all again to plug more profit leaks. Think back over what worked well the first time and do more of that. As you begin again:

> ✔ What are the steps?
> ✔ How are the steps actionable and verifiable?
> ✔ How can they be automated?
> ✔ What reminders or tools can be put in place?

Take the time to note what worked well in your first run through the PEAK program, how well your data supported the effort, how your team came together, how business processes affected each other, and any other reactions. By carefully analyzing your experience, you can build a sustainable review process to use any time you want to plug profit leaks. Based on your lessons learned, it gets faster and easier each time. You'll have the beginnings of a PEAK profit system that keeps your business humming along reaching Peak Profit Potential.

Six characteristics of successful systems are shown in the diagram.

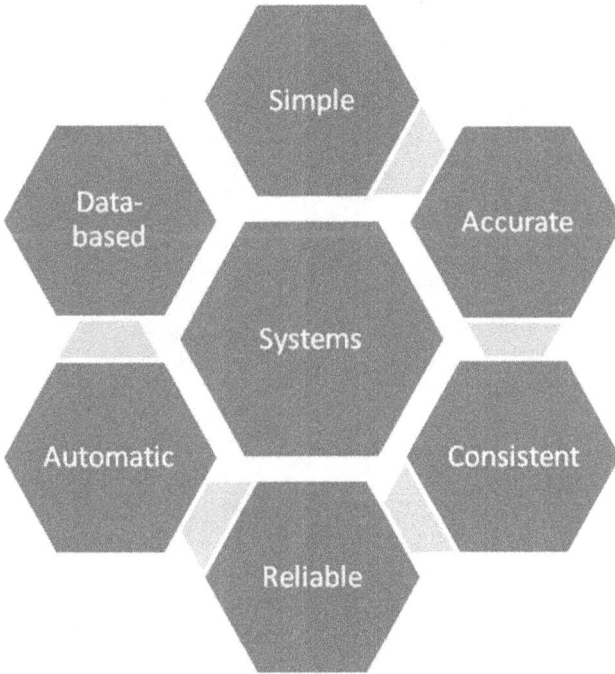

Other attributes include that it can be overridden by exception, there are methods to catch and flag exceptions, and it is possible to track important trends. What characteristics of successful systems are included in your PEAK action plan?

CHAPTER 12

NEXT STEPS

Mastery is a mindset: It requires the capacity to see your abilities not as finite, but as infinitely improvable. Daniel Pink

The PEAK program provides a powerful framework that is both simple and effective. By applying the program in your business you can produce amazing results on your bottom line. The first time around is the most important as you learn more about your business from the inside out, where the data is available and where it is not, and how to engage with outside help from your accountant, banker, or other trusted source.

Complete the PEAK analysis from end to end for your #1 profit leak. Identify your options, select a path, and make the needed changes. Review and test the changes closely; your business is an interlocking network. Many processes in your business affect many other processes; some in not so obvious ways. After you systematize the changes, it's important to continue to monitor them. Measure the profit impact. Document the profit impact. Measure other changes in cycle time, quality, and customer service. Note the lessons learned about your business and about the PEAK 4-step program. When you have verified information ready to share, circulate the results widely so that everyone involved knows what you're doing and why you're doing it.

The Power of Data

There are some things that only you know about your business. It's important to stay fully involved in the early days of the PEAK program to recognize the full potential of detailed information and the ways in which it can be used to help you manage your business. You'll see the power of data and actionable information in action. After you fully appreciate what data is possible to produce, you can use it to make better decisions in many areas of your business. After the initial design and implementation efforts are running smoothly you can step back and play a supporting role.

… There are dozens of areas in a small business where **major profits leaks can occur** …

Just don't step back too far. It's your business after all – you have the most at stake. You have the most to gain and the most to lose. Over time you'll find the right balance of what to do. The trick is to know that when someone tells you something that sounds off, you have a sense of where to look to verify it. To get to the bottom of it.

Do the PEAK program again for your #2 profit leak. Take due care to fully explore the second profit leak. This leak might be completely different from the first leak that you plugged so use the same systematic methodology to seek out essential information and find out what's going on in this next area of your business. Does the potential leak relate to a specific product or service? Is it an internal process that's taking too much time? Does it consistently have a negative impact on quality? Are a certain group of customers increasing your costs more than you expected? Are some suppliers falling down on their promises for quality, quantity, or timeliness? Is the cost of credit an issue where slow payers are causing an unexpected cash squeeze for your business? There are dozens of areas in a small business where major profit leaks can occur. These questions only scratch the surface of what is going on in your business. Frame your own questions and go get started.

Integrate the PEAK methodology into your quarterly and annual review of your business. Did I just hear you say; "What quarterly review of my business?" If you don't do one, you're like 71% of all businesses that don't do quarterly reviews unless they're forced to by their bankers or investors. Begin to do more interim reviews of your business and track the trends; once a year is not nearly enough to help you manage your business. And it's far too late to stop profit leaks before they cost you a small fortune. Systematically manage your business. Keep at it and you'll reap the rewards.

If you don't believe me, here's a challenge. Contrast the impact of plugging a $100 profit leak with the impact of increasing sales by $100. The extra $100 in sales generates profits at your profit margin rate, let's say 15%. So a $100 sale might generate an extra $15 in gross profit. Plugging a $100 profit leak results in $100 being added directly to the bottom line. Isn't $100 added to your bottom line better than $15? Plugging your profit leaks is low-hanging fruit. It's time to pick it before it falls off the tree and through your hands.

Play to your strengths. Rigorously monitor business operations and product quality to boost your profits and enhance customer value. Examine where you are delivering the best customer service. Now make it better by making it easier for your customers to work with you. My company slogan is *"Just Say No to the Status Quo*™. Don't be afraid to shake things up a little or a lot as long as you're doing it with current and future customers in mind. Get the core processes working efficiently and effectively, then look for ways to make them better and faster – from your customer's perspective. Your activities are designed to build customer trust so that they're ready to do more and bigger business deals with you.

One powerful way for your customers to show their satisfaction and loyalty with your company is to give you testimonials; it's huge for building your credibility. A thank you letter from a customer, a list of customers willing to provide references, and pictures of satisfied customers on your website show that others have bought your product or service and are really satisfied.

After you plug the three top profit leaks in your business you're ready for Continuous Profit Maximization. And the good news is that you can run through the 4-step PEAK program again and again to plug your major profit leaks one right after another. And to keep them plugged once and for a all.

* * *

The next chapter presents an optional analysis of you and your core values for your business. If you always know why you do the things you do and you are very satisfied with the outcomes, then skip on to the chapter entitled **Continuous Profit Maximization**. If on the other hand, you are like most small business owners and entrepreneurs, over time things have shifted. You are working

longer and harder and the financial freedom and schedule flexibility that you were seeking has proven to be more elusive than
you expected. A core values assessment might be just the activity you need to get your energy and focus back. Give it a try…you
have nothing to lose and everything to gain.

CORE VALUES FOR YOUR BUSINESS

We do not act rightly because we have virtue or excellence, but we rather have those because we act rightly. Aristotle

This chapter presents an analysis of what core values you hold for your business. It always leads to discoveries and often to some big surprises. This exercise can be done in every aspect of your life, but for our purposes here, please focus only on you and your business values. Not as a spouse, or parent, or citizen, or member of your community...but as a business person. The values that you embody in your business are clearly visible to your customers – even if they are not so obvious to you. That will change soon. You can also find this values list on the book website at *http://www.PeakProfitPotential.com*.

___ **Step 1:** Go through the list and **underline** your 15 most important business values.

✔ **Step 2:** Review the list of underlined values and check your top 10 business values.

O **Step 3:** Review your checkmarks and circle your top 5 business values.

Business Values List

Action-oriented	Dedicated	Honesty	Problem solving
Accomplishment	Dependability	Honor	Professionalism
Accountability	Determination	Hopeful	Punctuality
Achievement	Discipline	Imagination	Quality
Adaptability	Effectiveness	Independence	Reasonableness
Accuracy	Efficiency	Insight	Recognition
Appreciation	Empathy	Integrity	Resilience
Awareness	Encouragement	Intelligence	Resourcefulness
Boldness	Energetic	Intuition	Respect
Candor	Enjoyment	Justice	Security
Caring	Enthusiasm	Kindness	Self-reliance
Character	Equality	Knowledge	Sensitivity
Cheerfulness	Environment	Leadership	Sincerity
Clarity	Ethical	Learning	Strength
Coherence	Excellence	Loyalty	Stability
Commitment	Fairness	Meaningful	Teaching
Communication	Fearlessness	Motivation	Timely
Community	Flexibility	Nimbleness	Tolerance
Compassion	Frankness	Nobility	Toughness
Confidence	Freedom	Objectivity	Trustworthy
Connection	Free-thinking	Openness	Truthful
Consciousness	Fulfillment	Optimism	Understanding
Conservation	Fun	Organized	Understated
Cooperation	Gallantry	Passion	Uniqueness
Courage	Generosity	Planning	Unity
Courtesy	Giving	Performance	Vision
Creativity	Goodwill	Perseverance	Voice
Credibility	Gratitude	Persistence	Wisdom
Curiosity	Harmony	Practicality	Other
Decisiveness	Helpful	Precision	Other

After you have your five business values selected, consider these questions. These five values are the strongest ones that you selected after eliminating all of the other values. Why?

What do these 5 values mean to you?

_____

_____

Which values did you expect to be included?

_____

_____

Which business values surprised you?

_____

_____

What actions will you take based on these values?

_____

_____

CHAPTER 14

CONTINUOUS PROFIT MAXIMIZATION

We are what we repeatedly do. Excellence, then, is not an act, but a habit. Aristotle

To reach your Peak Profit Potential, fervently adopt a mindset that focuses on continuous profit maximization. Why not keep more of what you earn? Plugging profit leaks is an incredible, yet often overlooked way to boost your profits on a continuous basis.

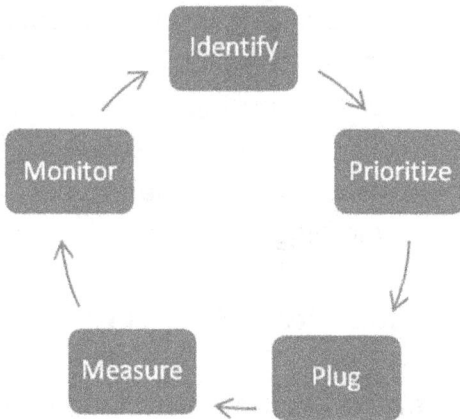

Going Forward

Designing and testing your performance measurement system is an important first step. A very important step indeed, but it's just the beginning. Look back over your high priority profit leaks and review the tools and ratios that provide insights for you to make faster, better, more-informed business decisions. If you prefer, look into one area of your business at a time, one level at a time to identify areas to drive additional customer value. They're all around you. Profitability is just a like a seed; there is so much potential in your business. Geoffrey Chaucer inspired us with the vision that from the simple acorn grows the mighty oak. Tend to your business, nurture it, shape it, and watch your profits grow. You already have everything you need.

Redefine major processes in your business to build in excellence and then measure, measure, measure. Build a simple system that runs automatically at the end of each month. Continuously evaluate your performance measures. What are they really telling you? What are you learning about your business from each of your measures? Is there something else you need to know or are these measures giving you the full, accurate picture? Keep in mind that improved performance measures lead to increased profits in your business. So don't marry your measures; keep improving them for even bigger payoffs.

Your New Perspective

Look back and review how you implemented the 4-step PEAK program. How did it work in your business? What changes are needed? Are you delivering excellence? Are your measures and exception reports getting closer to where you want them to be or are they still somewhat off the mark? Don't be surprised by how much your perspective is changing as your performance management experience grows. You can now view your performance measures in the overall context of your business. When you're fully satisfied that you're actually measuring what you think you are, systematize your measures so they are generated automatically. Don't leave systematic tracking of your performance measures to chance. Have them appear automatically on your screen around the first of each month and take the time to review the exceptions and trends carefully.

After you're satisfied that your measures are just what you need, continue looking for the next most productive areas for profit leaks in your business. Where are there hidden costs that might lead to hidden profit opportunities? Each area has significance for your business. Select an area to explore and go systematically through the 4-step PEAK program. It gets easier each time and it's very rewarding to go deep into your business with an analytical mindset, ratcheting up performance, enhancing customer value, and boosting profits.

Profit maximization is an important business objective. It can be started and stopped as needed or run continuously based on the needs of your business over time. Sometimes seasonal factors force you to focus solely on production. When that happens, and it's determined to be the best use of your time from the customer value perspective, then by all means do that.

Periodic Reviews

Many businesses get their operations on solid profit footing and then consistently reevaluate them each quarter. When any major profit leaks or business process events present themselves, jump on them as soon as you can. Measurement shouldn't interfere with running your business; in fact, it's an essential part of running your business. Measurement and change are not ends in themselves. Each new performance measure must prove its value to your business. And it must be doable. It must be scalable. And it must add value in terms of excellent customer service, profitability, or both.

> ... *Measurement shouldn't interfere with running your business; it's an* **essential part** *of running your business ...*

Change for Profit's Sake

Change can be quite disruptive so take a break when you need one. Fully implementing one measure is far more important than creating multiple new incomplete and untested measures. The Hippocratic oath in medicine cautions to first do no harm. The same caution applies in business. Make only needed, proven changes to the ways you measure performance in your business. Then do it again and again at your own pace, as needed, as warranted.

Start in a new area. Plug the leaks. Keep it going. Measure and report. Prevent future leaks in the same area. Many times one area will illuminate another. This is where the fun comes in when you think the problem is in one place but instead it's located in the step before or the step after. Dig deeper and drill down. You're mining for hidden profits and there is pure gold there when you plug a persistent profit leak.

It's worth the effort and you'll learn so much about how your business works. You'll become intimately familiar with your cost drivers, profit drivers, and value drivers. Many business owners create new products from what they learn. Over time business processes get old but often we just keep on doing things the way we have always done them, to the detriment of our profits. Taking a closer look can open up new avenues with very little effort and resources.

Keep an open mind, not all customers are alike; not all customer needs are alike all the time. Some customers might pay more for faster delivery in some cases, but not always. Others might pay more for drop shipping to multiple locations. Still others might pay for higher quality or simple product modifications. Looking into and fully costing your business processes can present you with a myriad of feasible and profitable options for you to consider. Analytically without emotion. Data-based decisions without haste. Business intelligence enables you to take back your power. Implement one or two, or none of the options. Base your decisions on performance measures that track customer value and excellence to reach your Peak Profit Potential.

Your Profit Strategy

Now is the time to become strategic about profits in your business. Take your top three ideas and evaluate them with your eye on exceptional customer value and profitability targets. You now have a little more time and space to take a new look to broaden or deepen your offerings in ways that will increase your profit potential. As you explore what else you could be doing, remember that everything has an opportunity cost. When you're doing one thing you're not doing something else.

To review, each hour has a cost and each hour also has an intrinsic value. Evaluate business processes and activities with the best value of an hour in mind. (For an interesting video on the Value of an Hour, go to *www.PeakProfitPotential.com/valuehour.*) As CEO, you are responsible for sales, strategy, product development, production, customer service, financing and many more activities. Keep profits in mind for both the business as it looks today and for how you want it to look in the future. Every business process can be viewed in the context of six factors that are required to make it successful.

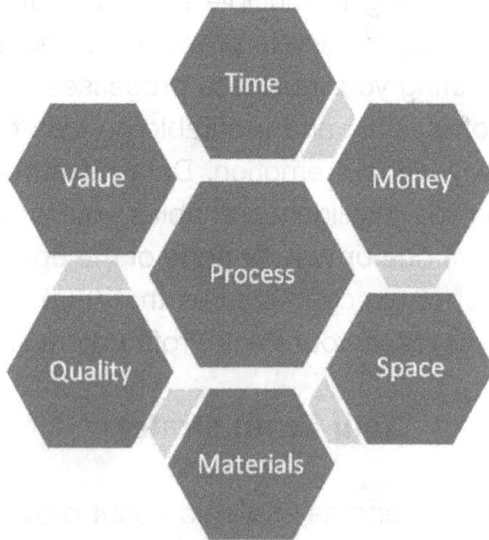

The New View

When your business is running like a finely tuned profit machine, it's time to reap the rewards. You'll have more time to focus your strategic attention because you have eliminated unnecessary and unproductive activities all throughout your business that have dominated your operational attention up until now. You'll have more satisfied customers because everything you do focuses on increasing customer value. You'll have more profits because increasingly meeting customer needs builds loyalty and customer retention, referrals, and reduces the cost of new customer acquisition.

Doing the right things right drives profits in your business. And as you have seen, it's easy to get started in the first area in your business. The sooner you start, the sooner you'll reap the rewards. Tangible rewards. Profits. And intangible rewards. An analytical mindset focused on performance measurement to drive customer value. You don't need to go all geek, although you could. It's that much fun once you get started. For the majority of business owners just a few simple changes show astonishing results. They reveal hidden profits right under your feet.

No magic bullet. Just powerful tools and techniques that you can do yourself. No long-term contracts or switching fees. No minimum balance. No long-term consulting fees. Your old performance measures can be banished and replaced with new, more effective ones whenever you're ready to get started. How about now? Isn't now a good time for you to reach your Peak Profit Potential?

CHAPTER 15

MAIN MESSAGES OF PEAK PROFIT POTENTIAL

*Our goal is long-term growth in revenue and absolute profit...
so we invest aggressively in future innovation while tightly
managing our short-term costs. Larry Page*

The Main Messages of Peak Profit Potential

The major peak profit potential themes from the research,
analysis, and implementation experience are:

- ✔ Getting started now to reach your Peak Profit Potential
  is more important than doing it perfectly.
- ✔ Doing the right things right is far more important than
  doing everything.
- ✔ Delivering exceptional customer value at a profit is the
  core of your business.
- ✔ Every business is unique, yet a few key indicators can
  guide decision making in every business to maximize
  profits.
- ✔ What you don't know can seriously harm your business. Assumptions are often both wrong and costly.

✔ Get the help you need for as long as you need it.

✔ Balance your strategic attention and your operational attention over the course of each month.

✔ Focus on just a few performance measures. Test them, refine them, and track them.

✔ Performance management is a continuous process. You can always reap more benefits no matter how well your business is running.

✔ Adopt a continuous profit maximization mindset for yourself and coach your team on the 4-step PEAK program.

✔ Work with your customers early and often to keep things running smoothly and profitably and to better understand their needs.

✔ Track your costs actively or they could expand in direct proportion with volume or erode your profit margins.

CHAPTER 16

IMPLEMENTATION STARTS HERE

On your mark, ready, set, action!

You've seen the tools. You've read the cases. You've seen the results. You've felt the excitement when things fell into place for a successful business owner.

The tools work, no matter the size of the business, no matter the industry. They help to cut excess costs. They help to boost profits.

The preparation phase is over. Now it's your turn. Take the assessments. The key steps are to: identify, design, and implement with directed action. Then test the results and do it again.

Join one of my implementation programs to get on-going guidance at *http://www.PeakProfitPotential.com*

ASSESSMENTS

How to Use These Assessments

To short cut the process of applying **The Profit Pyramid**™ in your business right away I've added a few sample assessment sheets that will start you thinking about what is happening in key areas of your business. They are also available online at *http://www.PeakProfitPotential.com*

The Purpose

These are just ideas and this is just a start. I invite you to go first through these assessments as they are, then think of new areas to explore or areas where it would it make sense to drill down in your business.

Feel free to add new topics, new activities, and new sheets to better align with your business and your analyses.

I invite your comments: Let me know how they are working for you and what else you need to succeed.

Your Business Profile

Total # of Products/Services

Top 3 Products/Services by Revenue
1._____
2._____
3._____

Top 3 Products/Services by Profit
1._____
2._____
3._____

Total # of Customers

Top 3 Customers by Revenue
1._____
2._____
3._____

Top 3 Customers by Profit
1._____
2._____
3._____

Baseline Operational Assessment

Date_____

1. What was your overall profit margin % over the past 2 years?

   _____

2. What is your #1 profit challenge?

   _____

3. Is this a temporary profit challenge?

   _____

4. How long has it been a profit challenge?

   _____

5. How does this profit challenge affect your business?

   _____

6. What have you tried in the past to overcome this?

   _____

7. What has worked?

   _____

8. What hasn't worked?

   _____

9. What could you do if this profit challenge was resolved?

   _____

10. What information or help do you need to proceed?

    _____

Baseline SWOT Analysis

Strengths

What are the 5-top strengths in your business? Here are a few examples, fill in your own.

Increasing sales
Increasing profits
New product pipeline
Strweamlined processes
Skilled team
Solid systems
Solid customers

1. _____

2. _____

3. _____

4. _____

5. _____

Baseline SWOT Analysis

Weaknesses

What are the 5-top weaknesses in your business? Here are a few examples, fill in your own.

Aging products
Declining sales
Profit squeezes
High fixed costs
Unclear start
Expensive rework

1. _____

2. _____

3. _____

4. _____

5. _____

ASSESSMENTS

Baseline SWOT Analysis

Opportunities

What are the 5-top opportunities for your business? Here are a few examples, fill in your own.

Partners
Innovation
Technology
New markets
New materials
New supply chains

1. _____

2. _____

3. _____

4. _____

5. _____

Baseline SWOT Analysis

Threats

What are the 5-top threats for your business? Here are a few examples, fill in your own.

Competition
Product obsolescence
Cost to acquire a customer
Economy
Falling demand
Price pressures
Financing gaps

1. _____

2. _____

3. _____

4. _____

5. _____

Baseline Business Strategy Assessment

Date: _____

On a scale of 1-10, please rate the following:

How well does your strategy:

1. Clearly, consistently focus your efforts? ___
2. Inform your customers about your business? ___
3. Inform the marketplace? ___
4. Accommodate growth and change? ___
5. Directly guide customer value creation? ___
6. Directly lead to product development? ___
7. Align with your current priorities? ___
8. Remain stable and not overly -reactive? ___
9. Vet new information under consideration? ___
10. Outline what you don't do? ___

Total score ___

Total score is the current % of alignment with your strategy.

What is your reaction to your results: _____
_____
_____

1-Month Business Strategy Assessment

Date: _____

On a scale of 1-10, please rate the following:

How well does your strategy:

1. Clearly, consistently focus your efforts?   ____
2. Inform your customers about your business?   ____
3. Inform the marketplace?   ____
4. Accommodate growth and change?   ____
5. Directly guide customer value creation?   ____
6. Directly lead to product development?   ____
7. Align with your current priorities?   ____
8. Remain stable and not overly -reactive?   ____
9. Vet new information under consideration?   ____
10. Outline what you don't do?   ____

Total score   ____

Total score is the current % of alignment with your strategy.

What is your reaction to your results: _____
_____
_____

2-Month Business Strategy Assessment

Date: _____

How well does your strategy:

1. Clearly, consistently focus your efforts? ___

2. Inform your customers about your business? ___

3. Inform the marketplace? ___

4. Accommodate growth and change? ___

5. Directly guide customer value creation? ___

6. Directly lead to product development? ___

7. Align with your current priorities? ___

8. Remain stable and not overly -reactive? ___

9. Vet new information under consideration? ___

10. Outline what you don't do? ___

Total score ___

Total score is the current % of alignment with your strategy.

What is your reaction to your results: _____

_____

_____

Baseline Goals and Objectives Assessment

Date: _____

On a scale of 1-10, please rate the following:

1. How close are you to your profit goals? ___
2. How close are you to growth goals? ___
3. How close are you to your income goals? ___
4. How close are you to your lifestyle goals? ___
5. How close are you to your market positioning goals? ___
6. How close are you to your prospecting goals? ___
7. How close are you to your prospect conversion goals? ___
8. How close are you to your decision making goals? ___
9. How close are you to your business process goals? ___
10. How close are you to your systems and data goals? ___

Total score ___

Total score is the current % of alignment with your goals & objectives.

What is your reaction to your results: _____
_____
_____

1-Month Goals and Objectives Assessment

Date: _____

On a scale of 1-10, please rate the following:

1. How close are you to your profit goals? ___

2. How close are you to growth goals? ___

3. How close are you to your income goals? ___

4. How close are you to your lifestyle goals? ___

5. How close are you to your market positioning goals? ___

6. How close are you to your prospecting goals? ___

7. How close are you to your prospect conversion goals? ___

8. How close are you to your decision making goals? ___

9. How close are you to your business process goals? ___

10. How close are you to your systems and data goals? ___

Total score ___

Total score is the current % of alignment with your goals & objectives.

What is your reaction to your results: _____

_____

_____

2-Month Goals and Objectives Assessment

Date: _____

On a scale of 1-10, please rate the following:

1. How close are you to your profit goals? ___

2. How close are you to growth goals? ___

3. How close are you to your income goals? ___

4. How close are you to your lifestyle goals? ___

5. How close are you to your market positioning goals? ___

6. How close are you to your prospecting goals? ___

7. How close are you to your prospect conversion goals? ___

8. How close are you to your decision making goals? ___

9. How close are you to your business process goals? ___

10. How close are you to your systems and data goals? ___

Total score ___

Total score is the current % of alignment with your goals & objectives.

What is your reaction to your results: _____

_____

_____

Baseline Sales and Marketing Assessment

Date: _____

On a scale of 1-10, please rate the following:

1. Overall Sales Level and Trend ___

2. Building a Prospect Funnel ___

3. Prospect Management ___

4. Sales Close Ratio ___

5. Cost of Making a Sale ___

6. Marketing Program Reach ___

7. Marketing Program Return ___

8. Advertising and Promotion ___

9. Market Research ___

10. New Market Identification ___

Total score ___

Total score is the current % of adequacy of your sales & marketing activities.

What is your reaction to your results: _____

_____

_____

2-Month Sales and Marketing Assessment

Date: _____

On a scale of 1-10, please rate the following:

1. Overall Sales Level and Trend   ____
2. Building a Prospect Funnel   ____
3. Prospect Management   ____
4. Sales Close Ratio   ____
5. Cost of Making a Sale   ____
6. Marketing Program Reach   ____
7. Marketing Program Return   ____
8. Advertising and Promotion   ____
9. Market Research   ____
10. New Market Identification   ____

Total score   ____

Total score is the current % of adequacy of your sales & marketing activities.

What is your reaction to your results: _____
_____
_____

Baseline Financial Management Assessment

Date: _____

On a scale of 1-10, please rate the following on adequacy:

1. Long-term Capital ____

2. Working Capital ____

3. Line of Credit ____

4. Cash Flow ____

5. Cash Management ____

6. Receivables Management ____

7. Payables Management ____

8. Debt Management ____

9. Equity Management ____

10. Tax Management ____

Total Score ____

Total score is the current % of adequacy of your financial management on these dimensions.

What is your reaction to your results: _____
_____
_____

2-Month Financial Management Assessment

Date: _____

On a scale of 1-10, please rate the following on adequacy:

1. Long-term Capital ____
2. Working Capital ____
3. Line of Credit ____
4. Cash Flow ____
5. Cash Management ____
6. Receivables Management ____
7. Payables Management ____
8. Debt Management ____
9. Equity Management ____
10. Tax Management ____

Total Score ____

Total score is the current % of adequacy of your financial management on these dimensions.

What is your reaction to your results: _____
_____
_____

Financial Measures Assessment

What financial measures do you currently use in your business?

1. Current Ratio

2. Quick Ratio

3. Average Collection Period

4. Cash Flow Margin

5. Inventory Turnover

6. Profit Margin

7. Gross Profit Margin

8. Operating Profit Margin

9. Debt Ratio

10. Return on Equity

What is your view on the overall effectiveness of your financial measures?

_____

_____

Non-Financial Measures Assessment

What non-financial measures do you currently use in your business?

1. Prospect quality

2. Customer buying patterns

3. Customer purchase history

4. Brand awareness

5. Quality measures

6. Repeat business drivers

7. Partner satisfaction

8. Partner effectiveness

9. Willingness to give referrals

10. Other

What is your view on the overall effectiveness of your non-financial measures?

_____

_____

APPENDIX

Top 10 Risks in Small Business

1. Lack of demand or sales

2. Lack of financing and cash

3. Lack of prospects in the sales funnel

4. Undifferentiated products

5. Low price is the leading strategy

6. Reliance on 1 or 2 main customers

7. Excess facility costs

8. Excess capital equipment costs

9. Unresolved customer complaints

10. Rework due to variable and unreliable quality

Top 10 General Profit Killers

1. Excess purchasing

2. Facility costs

3. Vehicle costs

4. Telecom and IT costs

5. Mishandling materials and waste

6. Returns and refunds

7. Supplier disruption

8. One-off special orders

9. Unresolved customer disputes

10. Warranty claims and after-sales servicing

Top 10 Business Process Profit Killers

1. Marketing

2. Purchasing

3. Design

4. Costing

5. Production

6. Rework

7. Acceptance

8. Collections

9. Warranty claims and after-sales servicing

10. Returns

Top 10 Cost Issues

1. Excess cost of capital and financing

2. Underestimating quality review costs post-production and rework

3. Underestimating contribution to overhead

4. Underestimating change order costs

5. Excess staff and labor costs compared to sales and production levels

6. Excess networking, training, and travel expenses

7. Underestimating labor costs of production

8. Underestimating material costs of production

9. Underestimating equipment costs of production

10. Excess capital equipment costs vs. volume

Top 10 Small Business Ratios

1. **Current Ratio =** $\dfrac{\text{Current Assets}}{\text{Current Liabilities}}$

Current Assets = Cash + Securities + Accounts Receivable
Current Liabilities = Notes Payable + Interest Due + Accounts Payable

2. **Quick Ratio** = $\dfrac{\text{Current Assets - Inventories}}{\text{Current Liabilities}}$

3. **Average Collection Period** = $\dfrac{\text{Receivables}}{\text{Sales per Day}}$

4. **Cash Flow Margin** = $\dfrac{\text{Cash Flow from Operating Cash Flows}}{\text{Net Sales}}$

5. **Inventory Turnover** = $\dfrac{\text{Cost of Goods Sold}}{\text{Average Inventory}}$

6. **Profit Margin** = $\dfrac{\text{Net Profit After Taxes}}{\text{Sales}}$

7. **Gross Profit Margin** = $\dfrac{\text{Sales - Cost of Goods Sold}}{\text{Net Sales}}$

8. **Operating Profit Margin** = $\dfrac{\text{Earnings Before Interest and Taxes}}{\text{Net Sales}}$

9. **Debt Ratio** = $\dfrac{\text{Total Debt}}{\text{Total Assets}}$

10. **Return on Equity** = $\dfrac{\text{Net Income After Taxes}}{\text{Total Equity}}$

Top 10 Tools for Small Business Management Reporting (in alphabetical order)

1. AccountEdge
2. Bookkeeper
3. Business2Go
4. Cougar Mountain
5. CYMA
6. DacEasy
7. NewSuite Small Business
8. Quickbooks Pro
9. Sage 50 Accounting
10. Simply Accounting

Top Business Intelligence Tools for the Big Boys (in alphabetical order)

1. Birst
2. IBM
3. Information Builders
4. Microsoft BI
5. Microstrategy
6. Oracle
7. QlikTech
8. SAP
9. SAS
10. Tableau

10 Illustrative Profit Margins* in Small Business Segments

1. Software 30-90%
2. Computers and electronics 50-55%
3. Lawyers 15-40%
4. Medical equipment suppliers 25-30%
5. CPAs 15-20%
6. Small manufacturing 14-18%
7. Insurance agencies 12-15%
8. Health practices 10-15%
9. Food processing 10-12%
10. Publishing 8-10%

One key variable: labor-intensive operations are expected to cause profit margins to fall when labor costs are high vs. a more technology-intensive operation.

*These margins are illustrative only. As you can imagine as a business owner, average profit margins vary widely even within the same business sub segment; many factors are involved. Nevertheless, they are illuminating. These were shown in Forbes Magazine 2/10/11:*The Most Profitable Small Businesses.*

10 P's of Effective Goal Setting

1. Priority – only very important goals

2. Proven - the approach leads to end game

3. Possible – attainable with stretch

4. Power – you can get it done

5. Permission – access, licensing, fees, rights

6. Pacing – when to start and finish this goal

7. Payoff – picture your new future

8. Plan - specific, time bound, step-by-step

9. Persistence – be in it to win it!

10. Path – identify workarounds for potential obstacles

10 Keys to Effective Decision Making

1. Record the symptoms

2. Note the interdependencies

3. Identify the potential causes

4. Note what has changed internally

5. Note what has changed externally

6. Evaluate list of possible solutions

7. Select the best solution and team

8. Articulate the desired results

9. Implement with care

10. Evaluate progress at first milestone, realign as needed

10 Steps to Drive Exceptional Customer Value

1. Know what they want, how much, and why

2. Know how much they'll pay for it

3. List viable options to provide solutions

4. Select best option, offering, and approach

5. Itemize your total costs and margins

6. Verify the benefits with customers

7. Develop pilot processes and systems

8. Deliver to your clients

9. Collect customer feedback and testimonials

10. Measure and realign as needed

Jay Abraham's 7 Steps to Get Your Business Unstuck

If being stuck is the problem, what does it mean to get your business unstuck?

1. **Break down your numbers**, not just month to month, year to date, and year to year, but also into categories like how many leads, how many new sales by product, average sale, and average product-source. Then, analyze any and all correlations, implications, and anomalies this data tells you.

2. **Have a systematic, strategic process in place** that is designed in a predictable, sustainable, and continuous manner to bring in prospects and first-time buyers, and keep advancing and enhancing them forward to recurring purchases in a predictable manner that you can look at your numbers today and accurately predict what your business will be like in ninety days. You're able to engineer specific, predictable growth year after year.

3. **Produce not just incremental gains but exponential gains year after year.** Harness the little understood power to drive multiplied sales and profits. For example, Costco realized it made more money from selling memberships than from selling goods in its stores. So it tailors its advertising and marketing to bring people back to keep up their memberships.

4. **Be clear about all of the factors that affect your business**, and you realize none of them are insurmountable. In fact, the vast majority can be improved upon. See the potential income in any business situation and how to make it work for you in a most enriching manner. For example, you find that you have one category of buyers ten times more likely than others, and if you approach them the right way, they are likely to buy seventeen times more than your average client.

5. **Understand your competitors' appeal, advantage, and differentiation in the market**—and you know how to pre-empt these advantages, or successfully counter-position yourself against them. You learn why certain consumers buy from your competitors and not from you, and you know how to change that.

6. **Know the alternative products and services that your prospects can buy in lieu of your products and services**, including taking no action at all. And you can prove to them that choosing you represents the most astute decision any buyer could make. You know how to motivate and persuade them to take action and make buying decisions.

7. **Incorporate growth thinking into everything you do**, every action you take, every investment you make, every contact you forge with your buyer or marketplace.

With permission. Copyright 2008: *The Sticking Point Solution*, www.abraham.com

MORE THAN 100 OF MY FAVORITE QUOTES

o *The only difference between successful people and unsuccessful people is extraordinary determination.* Mary Kay Ash

o *Unless you try to do something beyond what you have already mastered, you will never grow.* Ralph Waldo Emerson

o *Where you are headed is more important than how fast you are going. Rather than always focusing on what's urgent, learn to focus on what is really important.* Stephen Covey

o *When one door closes, another opens; but often we look so long at the closed door that we do not see the one which has opened for us.* Helen Keller

o *Successful people understand that you don't need to make things complicated.* Anne McKevitt

o *Nothing has ever been achieved by the person who says: It can't be done.* Eleanor Roosevelt o *The most successful people fail the most times, because they try everything.* Wes Hopper

o *Successful people are simply those with successful habits.* Brian Tracy

o *Real knowledge is to know the extent of one's ignorance.* Confucius

o *Motivation is what gets you started. Habit is what keeps you going.* Jim Rohn

o *Sometimes adversity is what you need to face in order to become successful.* Zig Ziglar

o *I think if you do something and it turns out pretty good, then you should go do something else wonderful, not dwell on it for too long. Just figure out what's next.* Steve Jobs

o *A mind saturated with fear of failure or images of unwanted results can no more accomplish, create, or produce anything of value than a stone can violate the law of gravity.* Bob Proctor

o *Being a professional is doing the things you love to do — even on the days you don't feel like doing it.* Julius Erving

o *Nothing great in life has ever been accomplished without enthusiasm.* Ralph Waldo Emerson o *Do what you can, with what you have, where you are.* Teddy Roosevelt

o *Do something every day that scares you.* Eleanor Roosevelt

o *Whether you think you can or think you can't, you're right.* Henry Ford

o *Time is a created thing. To say I don't have time, is like saying, I don't want to.* Lao-Tzu

o *Someday we'll look back on this and it'll all seem funny.* Bruce Springsteen

o *It does not matter how slowly you go so long as you do not stop.* Confucius

o *You have within you right now, everything you need to deal with whatever the world can throw at you.* Brian Tracy

o *I cannot give you the formula for success, but I can give you the formula for failure – which is: Try to please every-body.* Herbert Bayard Swope

o *Good judgment comes from experience, and often experience comes from bad judgment.* Rita Mae Brown

o *Nothing will ever be attempted if all possible objections must be first overcome.* Samuel Johnson o *If everybody is thinking alike, then somebody isn't thinking.* George S. Patton

o *Lost time is never found again.* Benjamin Franklin

o *Do not go where the path may lead, go instead where there is no path and leave a trail.* Ralph Waldo Emerson

o *Either you run the day or the day runs you.* Jim Rohn

o *It doesn't matter where you are coming from. All that matters is where you are going.* Brian Tracy

o *If you need me to motivate you, I probably don't want to hire you.* Daniel Pink

o *All of life is a constant education.* Eleanor Roosevelt

o *If there is an end for all we do, it will be the good achievable by action.* Aristotle

o *Beware the barrenness of a busy life.* Socrates

o *To be yourself in a world that is constantly trying to make you something else is the greatest accomplishment.* Ralph Waldo Emerson

o *Mistakes are the portals of discovery.* James Joyce

o *If you learn from defeat, you haven't really lost.* Zig Ziglar o *People grow through experience if they meet life honestly and courageously. This is how character is built.* Eleanor Roosevelt

o *If what you are doing is not moving you towards your goals, then it's moving you away from your goals.* Brian Tracy

o *Once we accept our limits, we go beyond them.* Albert Einstein

o *Eighty percent of your profits come from twenty percent of your customers.* Pareto Principle

o *If your dreams don't scare you, they are not big enough.* Ellen Johnson Sirleaf

o *It is better to live one day as a lion, than a thousand days as lamb.* Roman Proverb

o *When was the last time you did something for the first time?* Unknown

o *Our greatest glory is not in never failing, but in rising up every time we fail.* Ralph Waldo Emerson

o *Success is not final, failure is not fatal: it is the courage to continue that counts.* Jim Rohn

o *Every choice you make has an end result.* Zig Ziglar

o *Learn from the mistakes of others. You can't live long enough to make them all yourself.* Eleanor Roosevelt

o *If you chase two rabbits, you will lose both.* Native American Saying

o *Success depends upon previous preparation, and without such preparation there is sure to be failure.* Confucius

o *Do what you do so well that they will want to see it again and bring their friends.* Walt Disney

o *Best efforts will not substitute for knowledge.* W. Edwards Deming

o *Even a correct decision is wrong when it was taken too late.* Lee Iacocca

o *With the new day comes new strength and new thoughts.* Eleanor Roosevelt

o *Money often costs too much.* Ralph Waldo Emerson

o *..And the reason for their success was that they've had more experiences or they have thought more about their experiences than other people.* Steve Jobs

o *Time is the friend of the wonderful business, the enemy of the mediocre.* Warren Buffett

o *Don't limit yourself. Many people limit themselves to what they think they can do. You can go as far as your mind lets you. What you believe, remember, you can achieve.* Mary Kay Ash

o *A goal properly set is halfway reached.* Zig Ziglar

o *A lot of people are afraid to tell the truth, to say no. That's where toughness comes into play. Toughness is not being a bully. It's having backbone.* Robert Kiyosaki

o *Most new jobs won't come from our biggest employers. They will come from our smallest. We've got to do everything we can to make entrepreneurial dreams a reality.* Ross Perot

o *The most important single central fact about a free market is that no exchange takes place unless both parties benefit.* Milton Friedman

o *We see our customers as invited guests to a party, and we are the hosts. It's our job every day to make every important aspect of the customer experience a little bit better.* Jeff Bezos

o *Make your product easier to buy than your competition, or you will find your customers buying from them, not you.* Mark Cuban

o *Each time you learn something new you must readjust the whole framework of your knowledge.* Eleanor Roosevelt o *The aim of marketing is to know and understand the customer so well the product or service fits him and sells itself.* Peter Drucker

o *Your most unhappy customers are your greatest source of learning.* Bill Gates

o *This may seem simple, but you need to give customers what they want, not what you think they want. And, if you do this, people will keep coming back.* John Ilhan

o *I've learned that people will forget what you said, people will forget what you did, but people will never forget how you made them feel.* Maya Angelou

o *I'm able to serve my customer by knowing what she or he wants. People give me great ideas, tell me what they want, what they don't want.* Kathy Ireland

o *Spend a lot of time talking to customers face to face. You'd be amazed how many companies don't listen to their customers.* Ross Perot

o *There is only one boss. The customer. And he can fire everybody in the company from the chairman on down, simply by spending his money somewhere else.* Sam Walton

o *As you begin to take action toward the fulfillment of your goals and dreams, you must realize that not every action will be perfect. Not every action will produce the desired result. Not every action will work.* Jack Canfield o *An ounce of action is worth a ton of theory.* Ralph Waldo Emerson

o *Studies have shown that 90% of error in thinking is due to error in perception. If you can change your perception, you can change your emotion and this can lead to new ideas.* Edward de Bono

o *There is a certain degree of satisfaction in having the courage to admit one's errors. It not only clears up the air of guilt and defensiveness, but often helps solve the problem created by the error.* Dale Carnegie

o *Success seems to be connected with action. Successful people keep moving. They make mistakes, but they don't quit.* Conrad Hilton

o *Managers today have to do more with less, and get better results from limited resources, more than ever before.* Brian Tracy

o *You cannot change your destination overnight, but you can change your direction overnight.* Jim Rohn

o *In life and business, there are two cardinal sins. The first is to act precipitously without thought and the second is to not act at all.* Carl Icahn

o *I have to say I've made many mistakes, and been humbled many, many times. But you know what? It's never too late to learn.* Kathy Ireland o *Your best teacher is your last mistake.* Ralph Nader

o *One cannot too soon forget his errors and misdemeanors. To dwell long upon them is to add to the offense.* Henry David Thoreau

o *Experience is the name everyone gives to their mistakes.* Oscar Wilde

o *I've learned that mistakes can often be as good a teacher as success.* Jack Welch

o *I became successful due to several reasons. I never gave up and I never let anyone or anything get in my way. I use the power of positive thinking to tackle obstacles and challenges so they don't defeat me.* Lillian Vernon

o *Perseverance is failing nineteen times and succeeding the twentieth.* Julie Andrews

o *My best successes came on the heels of failures.* Barbara Corcoran

o *Advice is what we ask for when we already know the answer but wish we didn't.* Erica Jong

o *Never give up, for that is just the place and time that the tide will turn.* Harriet Beecher Stowe

o *You don't get paid for the hour. You get paid for the value you bring to the hour.* Jim Rohn o *In all realms of life it takes courage to stretch your limits, express your power, and fulfill your potential.* Suze Orman

o *We were most creative when our back was against the wall.* Anita Roddick

o *Decide what it is that you are and then stay true to that thing. My brand is based very much on how I live my day-to-day life.* Rachael Ray

o *I didn't get there by wishing for it or hoping for it, but by working for it.* Estee Lauder

o *My philosophy is that not only are you responsible for your life but doing the best at this moment puts you in the best place for the next moment.* Oprah Winfrey

o *Success is often achieved by those who don't know that failure is inevitable.* CoCo Chanel

o *Common sense is genius dressed in its working clothes.* Ralph Waldo Emerson

o *To think is easy. To act is difficult. To act as one thinks is the most difficult.* Johann Wolfgang Von Goeth

o *I like thinking big. If you're going to be thinking anything, you might as well think big.* Donald Trump

o *You get credit for what you finish, not what you start.* Unknown o *Shoot for the moon. Even if you miss, you'll land among the stars.* Les Brown

o *Every sale has five basic obstacles. No need, no money, no hurry, no desire, and no trust.* Zig Ziglar

o *Risk comes from not knowing what you're doing.* Warren Buffett

o *I feel that luck is preparation meeting opportunity.* Oprah Winfrey

o *A woman is like a tea bag; you never know how strong it is until it's in hot water.* Eleanor Roosevelt

o *Yesterday's home runs don't win today's games.* Babe Ruth

o *Winning is not a sometime thing; it's an all the time thing. You don't win once in a while, you don't do things right once in a while, you do them right all the time. Winning is habit. Unfortunately, so is losing.* Vince Lombardi

o *It is not the strongest of the species that survive, nor the most intelligent, but the one most responsive to change.* Charles Darwin

o *To be successful, you have to have your heart in your business, and your business in your heart.* Thomas Watson, Sr.

o *What could we accomplish if we knew we could not fail?* Eleanor Roosevelt o *Winners take time to relish their work, knowing that scaling the mountain is what makes the view from the top so exhilarating.* Denis Waitley

o *All life is an experiment. The more experiments you make the better.* Ralph Waldo Emerson

o *Having lost sight of our objective, we redoubled our efforts.* Unknown

o *The food is really bad, and such small portions!* Woody Allen

o *You must either modify your dreams or magnify your skills.* Jim Rohn

o *Miracles can be made, but only by sweating.* Giovanni Agnelli

o *Act as if what you do makes a difference. It does.* William James

o *Bad things aren't obvious when times are good.* Warren Buffett

o *Sometimes adversity is what you need to face in order to become successful.* Zig Ziglar

o *A stumbling block to the pessimist is a stepping-stone to the optimist.* Eleanor Roosevelt o   *The essence of a successful business is really quite simple. It is your ability to offer a product or service that people will pay for at a price sufficiently above your costs, ideally three or four or five times your cost, thereby giving you a profit...* Brian Tracy

o   *No matter what accomplishments you make, somebody helped you.* Althea Gibson

o   *Aerodynamically, the bumblebee shouldn't be able to fly, but the bumblebee doesn't know that, so it goes on flying anyway.* Mary Kay Ash

o   *Trying times are not the times to stop trying.* Ray Owen

o   *Nothing is more expensive than a missed opportunity.* H. Jackson Brown

o   *Chance favors those in motion.* James H. Austin

o   *In God we trust; all others bring data.* W. Edwards Deming

o   *Every successful man I have heard of has done the best he could with conditions as he found them, and not waited until the next year for better.* Edgar Howe

o   *I try to do the right thing at the right time. They may just be little things, but usually they make the difference between winning and losing.* Kareem Abdul-Jabbar o *Innovation is one percent genius and 99 percent hard work.* Peter Drucker

o *Either write something worth reading or do something worth writing.* Benjamin Franklin

o *The men/women who succeed are the efficient few. They are the few who have the ambition and will power to develop themselves.* Herbert N. Casson

o *If you want to live a happy life, tie it to a goal, not to people or things.* Albert Einstein

o *People do not decide to become extraordinary. They decide to accomplish extraordinary things.* Sir Edmund Hilary

o *The person who risks nothing, does nothing, has nothing, is nothing and becomes nothing.* Leo Buscaglia

o *Our aspirations are our possibilities.* Robert Browning

o *Learning is a treasure that will follow its owner everywhere.* Proverb

o *Trying times are not the times to stop trying.* Ray Owen

o *Vision without action is a daydream. Action without vision is a nightmare.* Japanese Proverb o *No matter what accomplishments you make, somebody helped you.* Althea Gibson

o *Aerodynamically, the bumblebee shouldn't be able to fly, but the bumblebee doesn't know that, so it goes on flying anyway.* Mary Kay Ash

BUSINESS DATA SOURCES

Here are five government sources of market data and statistics that may boost your market research efforts:

1. Business Data and Statistics from SBA.gov

For a good place to start go to *SBA.gov* and click on Business Data and Statistics, where you'll find a collection of resources providing free access to information about business and economic conditions and indicators collected by the U.S. government. Whether you sell to businesses or consumers, these sites include data and statistics on income, employment, trade, and manufacturing, and plenty more.

2. The U.S. Census Bureau

The U.S. Census Bureau (www.census.gov) maintains a vast repository of information that is quick and easy to navigate, thanks to a variety of Data Access Tools. For example, with The American FactFinder, just enter a city and state and the tool will generate multiple options for viewing social, economic, household and demographic data for your town or future location.

The main site has also been newly re-launched to make it very simple to find the data you need, including a neat interactive map that shows a mash-up of economic and demographic statistics for any town, city, or state in America.

If you like what you see but are not sure how to use and interpret the data, the Census Bureau hosts seminars across the country to help business owners learn more about business and industry data on the site.

3. FedStats.gov

If you want data but don't know which agency maintains or produces it, head on over to FedStats.gov. This no-frills data-driven site provides access to a full range of official statistical information produced by the federal government without having to know in advance which federal agency produces which particular statistic. Data is available on wide-ranging topics, including economic and population trends, crime, education, health care, aviation safety, energy use, and farm production.

4. Small Business Statistics

Interested in statistics about how small business is doing? The SBA Office of Advocacy conducts and publishes its own research on topics such as the small business economy.

5. EconomicIndicators.gov

For briefings on retail sales, durable goods, manufacturing, construction, new home sales, and more, Economicindicators.gov provides access to *daily* releases of key economic indicators from the Bureau of Economic Analysis and the Census Bureau. This is probably your best bet if you're looking for one site that says it all.

HOW TO USE THIS BOOK

It is the best of times; it is the worst of times to be in business. In some cases you are the product; you are the brand. In others, your brand is associated with your suite of offerings and your biggest customers. It can be quite exciting and somewhat daunting at the same time.

How you manage your business makes all the difference in the world to your profits. Are you constantly being pulled in five directions at once? Do you have too many clients or not enough? Are you making money on par with your efforts? Do you secretly wish for an 8-day week? Do you believe that your money is too tight right now for you to get some help?

The term "small business" is quite broad and can range from retail, manufacturing, consultants and coaches, to medical and legal practitioners, and beyond. Given the wide range of possibilities, the concepts in this book are necessarily industry independent, but nonetheless practical and important. As you peruse the ideas in this book, consider what is working well in your business and what is not. And also consider yourself. Are you looking for Change with a capital "C" or are you more comfortable now with small "c" change?

Do you routinely have large amounts of work left over at the end of the week? If so, as you know, it seriously affects your family time, your free time, and your mental outlook.

Well, there is good news and there is bad news.

The Opportunities and Challenges

From the perspective of opportunities, you have enhanced access to your local community; a simple search or targeted advertising can often identify hundreds of clients right in your neighborhood. And with a solid web page you can inform and screen potential clients to better guide them into your marketing plan if there is a match.

If you are a local provider, you can use videos, on-line training, VOIP, phone groups, and other techniques to give you access to far flung markets if you are interested. And if you choose to focus only on your local market these tools also work well in that environment to save you time and money, to increase productivity, as well as client satisfaction. When you need to be on-site that is where you will be. When you don't, at least you can explore the applicability of the alternatives.

Geographic boundaries for small businesses are falling every day. Well beyond your local market regional, national, and global best practices go viral in a flash. Depending upon your business, you can access wider markets and new classes of customers that were not either possible before or they were cost prohibitive. The new model is bricks and clicks.

In the business-to-consumer space, B2C, there is virtually un-limited potential. Many U.S. providers have new customers in Canada, UK, Australia, and India. This extensive reach is un-precedented for small business. Is it possible or desirable for you to tailor your offerings to have a wider appeal to wider markets? There are unparalleled opportunities that can take you away from exclusively on-site work and 1-on-1 client interactions. Even if your business is such that you need to be there, *e.g.* dentistry, be encouraged that there are tools to help increase your productivity.

From the perspective of challenges, there is boundless informa-tion available for free on the internet. At the same time of this ex-plosion of free material, many of the market leaders are coming down market from their Fortune 100 clients; it has now become cost-effective for them to market to small business. With the breakdown of barriers, you may be facing increased competition from unfamiliar competitors near and far, large and small.

Embrace the Change

Amazing market transformations are taking place across the spectrum and are accelerating rapidly. What worked three years ago – heck even one year ago - in small business marketing and delivery no longer works as well. Change is here now.

On a scale of 1-10 where are you and your business on change readiness?

Small business leaders of the future need to be proactive and agile, and adopt changes in their marketplace …. but only when

and if they make sense. The good news is that the upside is virtually unlimited because now you can take your small business well
beyond the local market and the nation using a variety of technology, tools, video, and online products.

Relevant Questions

Today the relevant questions are: Where are your skills and experience valued? Where can you make a difference and be a
market leader? And where can you effectively differentiate your
products and services for a profit?

The 4-step PEAK program presented in this book can make a
major difference in the way you:

- ✔ manage your business
- ✔ analyze your business
- ✔ drive profits to your bottom line.

Only you intimately know your business, what you have tried,
what has worked, and what has not worked in the past. So consider these secrets through the lens of your experience with your
business. And through your dreams for your business in the
future.

Clearly, one size does not fit all. All businesses and market conditions change over time. As you review the steps, consider how
they can apply to you in your business today. Some ideas dis-
cussed here might be very well suited for your business while
others might not be.

To make the most of this book keep an open mind. Consider the information that meets you where you are today in your business. Some ideas you will never take up; others you might take on later as you, your business, and the marketplace evolve. Not to worry, it's all good. The primary purpose is for you to think about your business in new and creative ways. *Creativity unleashes profitability.*

Managing Your Business

The 4-step PEAK program provides proven strategies and powerful tools you can use to align with your business plans. The ones that fit with your business as you have currently defined it will become part of your problem-solving arsenal that you can come back to again and again when meeting your profit goals really matters. When you follow proven formulas, you have the power to increase your profits. Turn that potential into reality now.

What is your schedule to implement the 4-step PEAK program?

Suggested Reading List

Jay Abraham. *The Sticking Point Solution: 9 Ways to Move Your Business from Stagnation to Stunning Growth In Tough Economic Times*, Vanguard Press, 2009

Steven M. Bragg. *Cost Reduction Analysis Tools and Strategies*, John Wiley & Sons, 2010

Jack Canfield. *The Success Principles(™): How to Get from Where You Are to Where You Want to Be,* Harper Collins, 2005

Gary Cokins. *Performance Management: Integrating Strategy Execution, Methodologies, Risk, and Analytics.* John Wiley & Sons, Inc. 2009.

Bill Collier. *How to Succeed as a Small Business Owner and Still Have a Life*, Porchester Press, 2006

Brenda Crompton & Robert Hubbs. *Leaking Money,* Infinitus Enterprises, 2011

Amy J.C. Cuddy, Matthew Kohut, John Neffinger. *Connect Then Lead*, Harvard Business Review, July-August 2013.

FG Crane. *Professional Services Marketing*, Haworth Press, 1993.

Michael E. Gerber. *The E Myth Revisited: Why Most Small Businesses Don't Work and What to Do About It,* Harper Business, 3rd edition, 1995

SUGGESTED READING LIST

Peter Guber. *Tell to Win*, Crown Business, 2011

Anne Hawkins. *100 Great Cost-Cutting Ideas*, Marshall Cavendish Business, 2010

Robin Hogarth and Emre Soyer. *A Picture's Worth a Thousand Numbers*, Harvard Business Review, June 2013.

Douglas W. Hubbard. *How to Measure Anything*, John Wiley & Sons, 2010

Adi Ignatius. *Strategy in a World of Flux*, Harvard Business Review, June 2013.

Michael G. Jacobides and John Paul MacDuffie. *How to Drive Value Your Way*, Harvard Business Review, July-August 2013.

Kaplan and Norton. The Balanced Scorecard: Translating Strategy into Action, Harvard Business School Press, Boston (1996)

Institute of Management and Administration. *Cost Reduction Best Practices*, 2nd edition, John Wiley & Sons, 2006

Seth Kahan, *Getting Change Right*. Jossey-Bass, 2010

Partick Lencioni. *The Advantage: Why Organizational Health Trumps Everything Else in Business*, Jossey-Bass, 2012

Jay and Jeannie Levinson. *Startup Guide to Guerilla Marketing*. Entrepreneur Press, 2008

Jim Loehr and Tony Schwartz. *The Power of Full Engagement*, Free Press, 2003

Nick Lovegrove and Matthew Thomas. *Triple-Strength Leadership*, Harvard Business Review, September 2013.

Perry J. Ludy. *Profit Building: Cutting Costs Without Cutting People*, Berrett-Koehler, 200

Michael Masterson. *Ready, Fire, Aim: Zero to $100 Million in No Time Flat*, Agora Press, 2008.

Daniel McGinn. *Inside Consulting's Black Box*, Harvard Business Review, September 2013.

Rita Gunther McGrath, *Transient Advantage*, Harvard Business Review, June 2013.

Lianabel Oliver. *The Cost Management Toolbox*, AMACOM, 2000.

Jim Palmer, *The Fastest Way to Higher Profits*, Success Advantage, 2011

Daniel H. Pink. *Drive: The Surprising Truth Behind What Motivates Us*, Riverhead Books, 2009

Michael Port. *Book Yourself Solid*. John Wiley & Sons, 2006.

Alex Rawson, Ewan Duncan, Conor Jones. *The Truth About the Customer Experience*, Harvard Business Review, September 2013.

SUGGESTED READING LIST

Cheryl L. Russell. *2001 Innovative Ways to Save Your Company Thousands*, Atlantic Publishing, 2007

Michael D. Ryall. *The New Dynamics of Competition*, Harvard Business Review, June 2013.

Bruce D. Schneider. *Energy Leadership: Transforming the Workplace and Your Life from the Core*, John Wiley & Sons, 2008

Brian Tracy. *Goals: How to Get Everything You Want - Faster Than You Ever Thought Possible,* Berrett-Koehler, 2010

Brian Tracy. *Maximum Achievement: Strategies and Skills That Will Unlock Your Hidden Powers to Succeed*, Fireside 1993.

Michael Treacy & Fred Wiersema. *The Discipline of Market Leaders*, Addison-Wesley, 1997

Price Waterhouse. *CFO: Architect of the Corporation's Future,* John Wiley & Sons, 1997

Andrew Wileman. *Driving Down Cost: How to Manage and Cut Costs Intelligently*, Nicholas Brealey Publishing, 2008

Wilkinghoff, Steve. *Found Money: Simple Strategies for Uncovering the Hidden Profit and Cash Flow in Your Business*, Wiley & Sons, 2009

David W. Young. *A Manager's Guide to Creative Cost Cutting*, McGraw-Hill, 2003

ABOUT THE AUTHOR

Dr. Donna Marie Thompson is a speaker and two-time best-selling author who has spent most of her 30-year career in international management consulting. She has helped scores of businesses to meet their strategic goals and profit targets under challenging circumstances. She was a Director at PricewaterhouseCoopers Consulting, and has worked at Booz Allen, as well as in small business consulting. She has the ability to break down complex problems into simple steps for analysis.

Donna Marie is a member of the National Speakers Association and as a platform speaker she has spoken to thousands in 11 countries. And as a cruise ship speaker, Donna Marie has toured the Caribbean and succeeded in teaching important concepts while having fun at the same time.

Donna Marie earned a PhD in International Business from George Washington University and an MBA from Virginia Polytechnic Institute. She has lectured on international business at the University of Maryland University College in the Executive MBA, on-line MBA, and on-site MBA programs. Donna Marie is a CPA, Certified Professional Coach, Certified NLP Practitioner, and Master Practitioner of the Energy Leadership Index.

Donna Marie is the President and CEO of Expert Profit Solutions with clients in the USA and abroad. Her wide range of experience in business leadership and strategy, performance management, and cost management uniquely qualifies her to guide firms to discover hidden profits.

Accomplishments

Donna Marie was recognized by America's Premier Experts in 2011 and was featured on the ION TV show "World's Greatest". She is currently the host of the **Business Bottom Line** radio show.

Donna Marie's motto is *Just Say No to the Status Quo*™

As a member of the Professional Woman Network she has co-authored three books, with another one on the way:

- ✔ *A View From the Top: Leadership Strategies for Women*
- ✔ *Breaking the Barriers: A Woman's Toolkit for Success*
- ✔ *The Confident Woman: Tapping Into Your Inner Power*
- ✔ *Coaching Gurus (coming soon)*

Dr. Thompson is an acclaimed speaker available for seminars, workshops, keynotes, and corporate training.

Contact:
Donna Marie Thompson, PhD
Expert Profit Solutions
301-312-7111
www.ExpertProfitSolutions.com
www.PeakProfitPotential.com

ABOUT EXPERT PROFIT SOLUTIONS

After several decades in Management Consulting for PricewaterhouseCoopers, Booz Allen, and local firms, Donna Marie Thompson formed Expert Profit Solutions to design practical tools to increase small business profitability. Her passion is for small business owners and entrepreneurs to create unmatched opportunities for financial independence. She scales tools that the big boys use to meet the needs of small businesses. Key focus areas are:

- ✔ Strategic Profitability Analysis
- ✔ Business Performance Measurement
- ✔ Strategic Business Expense Management

At Expert Profit Solutions, we:

- ✔ Conduct small business profitability assessments
- ✔ Conduct on line and on-site training programs
- ✔ Host multi-week intensive webinar series
- ✔ Lead multi-month profit implementation programs on line
- ✔ Offer multi-level membership programs to meet your needs
- ✔ Deliver keynote and platform speeches
- ✔ Conduct on-site workshops.

FOR MORE INFORMATION
ABOUT THE BOOK

Want to Know More?

To get more information about Peak Profit Potential, The Profit Pyramid™ and other Peak Profit Potential products and services, visit Donna Marie's book website at *www.PeakProfitPotential.com* where there is helpful information about:

- ✔ Interactive Book Discussions
- ✔ Chapter Working Groups
- ✔ Virtual Book Tour
- ✔ Peak Profit Potential Webinars
- ✔ Implementation Programs
- ✔ Weekend Programs
- ✔ Training and e-learning

To hire Donna Marie as a speaker for your organization go to *www.PeakProfitPotential.com*.

To buy this book in bulk for your company or organization, please leave a comment at *www.PeakProfitPotential.com/book*.

If you'd like to pose a question about the book go to *www.PeakProfitPotential.com/FAQ*. If you don't find the answer there, I encourage you to pose your question in the space provided and it will be added to the FAQs at a later date.

SOCIAL MEDIA CONTACTS

in Donna Marie Thompson

t ExpertProfits

f Donna Marie Thompson

EPS www.ExpertProfitSolutions.com

BONUS OFFER

If you are one of the many small business owners and entre-preneurs struggling to hit your stride in profitability, you may qualify for a free Profitability Assessment with Donna Marie using **The Profit Pyramid**™.

It's simple to qualify if you:

1) Own your own business
2) Formed before 2011
3) Are profitable as defined by revenues exceeding expenses
4) Are open to boosting your profits.

To see if you qualify for a free Profitability Assessment using **The Profit Pyramid**™ go to *www.PeakProfitPotential.com/assessment*

This could be just what you're looking for to turn your business around. Don't wait any longer to reach your Peak Profit Potential. Apply today!

www.ingramcontent.com/pod-product-compliance
Lightning Source LLC
Chambersburg PA
CBHW072301210326
41519CB00057B/2442